Weig_____ers®

Favou_____

Best-ever Chicken

SIMON &
SCHUSTER
ILLUSTRATED

London · New York · Sydney · Toronto · New Delhi

A CBS COMPANY

If you would like to find out more about Weight Watchers and the **ProPoints** Plan, please visit: www.weightwatchers.co.uk

🅥 This symbol denotes a vegetarian recipe and assumes that, where relevant, free range eggs, vegetarian cheese, vegetarian virtually fat free fromage frais, vegetarian low fat crème fraîche and vegetarian low fat yogurts are used. Virtually fat free fromage frais, low fat crème fraîche and low fat yogurts may contain traces of gelatine so they are not always vegetarian. Please check the labels.

❄ This symbol denotes a dish that can be frozen. Unless otherwise stated, you can freeze the finished dish for up to 3 months. Defrost thoroughly and reheat until the dish is piping hot throughout.

Recipe notes

Egg size: Medium, unless otherwise stated.

Raw eggs: Only the freshest eggs should be used. Pregnant women, the elderly and children should avoid recipes with eggs that are not fully cooked or raw.

All fruits and vegetables: Medium, unless otherwise stated.

Stock: Stock cubes are used in recipes, unless otherwise stated. These should be prepared according to packet instructions.

Recipe timings: These are approximate and meant to be guidelines. Please note that the preparation time includes all the steps up to and following the main cooking time(s).

Microwaves: Timings and temperatures are for a standard 800 W microwave. If necessary, adjust your own microwave.

Low fat spread: Where a recipe states to use a low fat spread, a light spread with a fat content of no less than 38% should be used.

Low fat soft cheese: Where low fat soft cheese is specified in a recipe, this refers to soft cheese with a fat content of less than 5%.

ProPoints values: Should you require the **ProPoints** values for any of the recipes within this book, you can call Customer Services on 0845 345 1500 and we will provide you with the relevant information on a recipe-by-recipe basis. Please allow 28 days for us to provide you with this information.

Contents

Introduction

Chicken – an incredibly versatile ingredient. From light bites to family favourites, speedy meals and special dishes for a dinner party, chicken is easy to cook and perfect in so many different recipes.

Add noodles and vegetables to create stir-fries such as Hoisin Chicken Noodles; stuff chicken breasts with garlic and soft cheese and roll them in breadcrumbs for Crispy Garlic Chicken Breasts; invite friends over for Italian style Pot Roast Chicken with Fennel or serve spicy Chicken and Vegetable Samosas when the neighbours pop round for a drink. You'll find ideas for lunches to take to work and lots of ways to use up leftovers from the Sunday roast, as well as supper dishes that you can get on the table quicker than you can say 'take-away'.

Chicken goes with anything and all these recipes are absolutely delicious and easy to follow. All you need to do is choose a recipe and get cooking your *Best-ever Chicken* recipes.

About Weight Watchers

For more than 40 years Weight Watchers has been helping people around the world to lose weight using a long term sustainable approach. Weight Watchers successful weight loss system is based on four tried and trusted principles:

- Eating healthily
- Being more active
- Adjusting behaviour to help weight loss
- Getting support in weekly meetings

Our unique **ProPoints** system empowers you to manage your food plan and make wise recipe choices for a healthier, happier you.

Storing and freezing

Many chicken dishes store well in the fridge, but make sure you use them up within a day or two. Some can also be frozen. However, it is important to make sure you know how to freeze safely.

- Wrap any food to be frozen in rigid containers or strong freezer bags. This is important to stop foods contaminating each other or getting freezer burn.
- Label the containers or bags with the contents and date – your freezer should have a star marking that tells you how long you can keep different types of frozen food.
- Never freeze warm food – always let it cool completely first.
- Never freeze food that has already been frozen and defrosted.
- Freeze food in portions, then you can take out as little or as much as you need each time.
- Defrost what you need in the fridge, making sure you put anything that might have juices, such as meat, on a covered plate or in a container.

- Fresh food, such as raw chicken, should be wrapped and frozen as soon as possible.
- Most fruit and vegetables can be frozen by open freezing. Lay them out on a tray, freeze until solid and then pack them into bags.
- Some vegetables, such as peas, broccoli and broad beans can be blanched first by cooking for 2 minutes in boiling water. Drain, refresh under cold water and then freeze once cold.

- Fresh herbs are great frozen – either seal leaves in bags or, for soft herbs such as basil and parsley, chop finely and add to ice cube trays with water. These are great for dropping into casseroles or soups straight from the freezer.

Some things cannot be frozen. Whole eggs do not freeze well, but yolks and whites can be frozen separately. Vegetables with a high water content, such as salad leaves, celery and cucumber, will not freeze. Fried foods will be soggy if frozen, and sauces such as mayonnaise will separate when thawed and should not be frozen.

Shopping hints and tips

Always buy the best ingredients you can afford. If you are going to cook healthy meals, it is worth investing in some quality ingredients that will really add flavour to your dishes. When buying meat, choose lean cuts of meat or lean mince, and if you are buying prepacked cooked sliced meat, buy it fresh from the deli counter.

When you're going around the supermarket it's tempting to pick up foods you like and put them in your trolley without thinking about how you will use them. So, a good plan is to decide what dishes you want to cook before you go shopping, check your store cupboard and make a list of what you need. You'll save time by not drifting aimlessly around the supermarket picking up what you fancy.

We've added a checklist here for some common storecupboard ingredients. Just add fresh ingredients to your regular shop and you'll be ready to cook your *Best-ever Chicken* recipes.

Storecupboard checklist

- [ ] apricots, dried ready to eat
- [ ] bay leaves
- [ ] black eyed beans, canned
- [ ] breadcrumbs, natural dried
- [ ] Cajun spice
- [ ] cannellini beans, canned
- [ ] cardamom pods
- [ ] chilli flakes
- [ ] chilli sauce
- [ ] Chinese five spice
- [ ] cinnamon, ground
- [ ] cloves
- [ ] cooking spray, calorie controlled
- [ ] coriander, ground
- [ ] cornflour
- [ ] couscous, dried
- [ ] cumin, ground
- [ ] curry (paste and powder)
- [ ] fish sauce
- [ ] flour, plain
- [ ] garam masala
- [ ] harissa paste

- [ ] herbs, dried (mixed and Italian)
- [ ] honey, clear
- [ ] jerk seasoning
- [ ] kidney beans, canned
- [ ] lentils, dried red
- [ ] lime leaves, dried
- [ ] mayonnaise, extra light
- [ ] mushrooms, dried porcini
- [ ] mustard (Dijon and wholegrain)
- [ ] noodles, dried
- [ ] oil (vegetable and olive)
- [ ] olives in brine, black
- [ ] paprika (regular and smoked)
- [ ] pasta, dried
- [ ] peppercorns
- [ ] pesto sauce
- [ ] pineapple, canned in natural juice
- [ ] raisins
- [ ] ras-el-hanout
- [ ] rice, dried (basmati and long grain)
- [ ] salt

- [ ] sesame seeds
- [ ] soy sauce
- [ ] stock cubes
- [ ] sweetcorn, canned
- [ ] tomato ketchup
- [ ] tomato purée
- [ ] tomatoes, canned
- [ ] turmeric
- [ ] vinegar (balsamic and wine)
- [ ] Worcestershire sauce

Soups and salads

Curried chicken soup

Serves 4
229 calories per serving
Takes 25 minutes to prepare,
   30 minutes to cook
❄

Yellow split peas thicken up this spicy chicken soup.

calorie controlled cooking
   spray

250 g (9 oz) skinless, boneless
   chicken breast, cut into
   chunks

1 large onion, chopped

1 large carrot, chopped finely

1 eating apple, unpeeled,
   cored and chopped

1 garlic clove, crushed

2 tablespoons tikka masala
   curry paste

2 tablespoons tomato purée

75 g (2¾ oz) dried yellow split
   peas

850 ml (1½ pints) chicken or
   vegetable stock

50 g (1¾ oz) frozen peas

2 tablespoons chopped fresh
   coriander

freshly ground black pepper

1 Heat a large lidded saucepan until hot and spray with the cooking spray. Gently fry the chicken for 2–3 minutes until lightly browned, then add the onion, carrot, apple and garlic and cook for another 1–2 minutes. Add the curry paste and fry gently for a few seconds.

2 Stir in the tomato purée, split peas and stock, then bring up to the boil. Reduce the heat, then cover and simmer for about 25 minutes or until the split peas are tender and the soup has thickened.

3 Add the peas and coriander. Simmer gently for another 2–3 minutes. Season to taste and then ladle the soup into warmed bowls. Serve immediately.

🅥 **Variation…** For a vegetarian version of this recipe, use vegetable stock and substitute 200 g (7 oz) Quorn Chicken Style Pieces for the chicken.

Simple chicken soup

Serves 4

155 calories per serving

Takes 10 minutes to prepare,
   40 minutes to cook

❅

*What could be more delicious than a bowl of chicken
soup? It's the ultimate comfort food.*

2 teaspoons vegetable oil

**165 g (5¾ oz) skinless,
   boneless chicken breast,
   chopped into small pieces**

**2 chicken stock cubes,
   dissolved in 1 litre (1¾ pints)
   hot water**

1 large onion, chopped finely

2 carrots, cubed

1 turnip, cubed

2 celery sticks, sliced finely

**2 tablespoons chopped fresh
   parsley**

50 g (1¾ oz) long grain rice

**salt and freshly ground black
   pepper**

1 Heat the vegetable oil in a large saucepan and add the
chicken. Cook for 3–4 minutes, stirring, until sealed and
browned.

2 Add all the remaining ingredients apart from the rice and
bring up to the boil. Reduce the heat and simmer gently,
partially covered, for 20 minutes.

3 Add the rice to the saucepan and cook for about 12–15
more minutes, or until the rice is tender.

4 Season the soup to taste, then ladle into warmed bowls
and serve at once.

Chicken soup with noodles

Serves 4

345 calories per serving

Takes 10 minutes to prepare,
  20 minutes to cook

❋

4 x 165 g (5¾ oz) skinless,
  boneless chicken thighs

2 teaspoons sunflower oil

1 garlic clove, crushed

2.5 cm (1 inch) fresh root
  ginger, peeled and grated

1 red chilli, de-seeded and
  finely chopped

850 ml (1½ pints) chicken
  stock

2 tablespoons soy sauce

2 tablespoons fresh lime juice

125 g (4½ oz) baby corn,
  trimmed

and halved

1 red pepper, de-seeded and
  cut into thin strips

6 spring onions, trimmed and
  shredded

125 g (4½ oz) thread egg
  noodles

2 tablespoons chopped fresh
  coriander

A fragrant filling Oriental soup with just a hint of chilli.

1 Grill the chicken thighs under a medium heat for 10 minutes until thoroughly cooked through. Allow to cool a little and then shred the meat finely by pulling it with two forks.

2 Heat the sunflower oil in a large pan and add the garlic, ginger and chilli. Cook for 1 minute and then add the shredded chicken, stock, soy sauce, lime juice, baby corn and red pepper.

3 Bring to the boil, reduce the heat and then simmer for 5 minutes. Add the spring onions and noodles to the pan. Cook for a further 5 minutes until the noodles are tender.

4 To serve, ladle into soup bowls and sprinkle with the chopped coriander.

Tip... The success of this soup really relies on the fresh herbs and spices that give a wonderful taste to the soup. However, you can use a teaspoon of dried chilli flakes if you don't have a fresh chilli to hand.

Chicken mulligatawny soup

Serves 8
145 calories per serving

Takes 15 minutes to prepare,
   25 minutes to cook

❄

**calorie controlled cooking
   spray**

2 large onions, cubed

4 carrots, cubed

**300 g (10½ oz) skinless,
   boneless chicken breast,
   sliced thinly**

4 garlic cloves, chopped

**2 tablespoons mild curry
   powder**

2 tablespoons tomato purée

**2 tablespoons smooth mango
   chutney**

**3 litres (5¼ pints) hot chicken
   stock**

125 g (4½ oz) basmati rice

*This is a filling and warming stew-style soup that tastes
great on winter days.*

1 Spray a large lidded saucepan with cooking spray and heat
until hot. Add the onions and carrots and cook, stirring for
3 minutes, until just tender. Add the chicken and garlic and
continue cooking for 2 minutes.

2 Stir in the curry powder, tomato purée and mango chutney.
Cook for 1 minute then add the stock and rice. Bring to the
boil, cover and simmer for 20 minutes until the vegetables
are tender and the rice is cooked.

3 Serve the soup in warm bowls.

Variation… This is a great way to use up leftover cooked
chicken. Remove the skin and just slice 215 g (7¼ oz)
cooked chicken thinly and add for the last 3–4 minutes
of cooking to heat through.

Asian chicken salad

Serves 1
320 calories per serving
Takes 25 minutes

100 g (3½ oz) cooked, skinless chicken breast
calorie controlled cooking spray
50 g (1¾ oz) carrots, grated
2 spring onions, sliced into long, thin strips
50 g (1¾ oz) fresh beansprouts
½ a small ripe mango, cubed
finely grated zest of ½ a lime
1 teaspoon crunchy peanut butter
1 teaspoon sweet chilli sauce
50 ml (2 fl oz) pineapple juice
¼ head of Chinese leaves, shredded

This stir-fry supper or snack for one is packed with fresh vegetables and fruit.

1 Use two forks to shred the chicken finely. Heat a non-stick frying pan and spray it with cooking spray. Add the chicken and stir fry for 3–4 minutes until it is heated through. Add the carrots, spring onions and beansprouts, and cook for a further 2 minutes, until the beansprouts have wilted a little.

2 Add the mango to the pan and stir well. Mix together the lime zest, peanut butter, chilli sauce and pineapple juice, and pour this into the pan. Stir well and cook for 2 minutes, until the sauce bubbles.

3 Arrange the shredded Chinese leaves on a serving plate and top with the hot chicken mixture.

Chicken, grape and potato salad

Serves 2
285 calories per serving
Takes 20 minutes

300 g (10½ oz) new potatoes, cubed

125 g (4½ oz) skinless, boneless chicken breast, halved horizontally

40 g (1½ oz) extra light mayonnaise

50 g (1¾ oz) low fat natural yogurt

1 tablespoon snipped fresh chives

½ teaspoon Dijon mustard (optional)

100 g (3½ oz) red seedless grapes, halved

1 Little Gem lettuce, leaves separated

freshly ground black pepper

This summery salad is a wonderful mixture of flavours and textures, brought together in a light, creamy dressing.

1 Bring a lidded saucepan of water to the boil and cook the potatoes, covered, for 15 minutes or until tender. Then drain them.

2 Meanwhile, heat the grill to medium high and grill the chicken for 10–12 minutes until cooked through. Set aside to cool.

3 In a large bowl, mix the mayonnaise with the yogurt, chives and mustard, if using, adding pepper to taste. Stir in the new potatoes and grapes. Slice the chicken and mix it into the potato salad. Serve on a bed of Little Gem lettuce leaves.

Variation… Try making this delicious potato salad with 125 g (4½ oz) skinless, sliced leftover roast chicken.

Quick chicken and sweetcorn soup

Serves 4
170 calories per serving
Takes 20 minutes
❄

326 g can sweetcorn, drained
2 chicken stock cubes,
dissolved in 1 litre (1¾ pints)
hot water
a pinch of dried chilli flakes
(optional)
1 tablespoon cornflour
150 ml (5 fl oz) skimmed milk
100 g (3½ oz) cooked, skinless
chicken, chopped
1 tablespoon chopped fresh
coriander or parsley, plus
coriander or parsley sprigs,
to garnish (optional)
salt and freshly ground black
pepper

Put this satisfying soup on the table in the time it takes
to brew a pot of coffee. Nearly all the ingredients are
storecupboard standbys.

1 Tip the sweetcorn into a large saucepan and add the chicken
stock and chilli flakes (if using). Bring up to the boil, then
reduce the heat and simmer for 10 minutes.

2 Transfer the mixture to a liquidiser or food processor and
blend for 15–20 seconds until smooth. Return the soup to the
saucepan.

3 Blend the cornflour with 2–3 tablespoons of the milk, then
stir into the saucepan with the remaining milk. Add the chicken
and coriander or parsley. Reheat, then season according to
taste.

4 Ladle the soup into warmed bowls and serve at once.
Garnish with coriander or parsley sprigs if desired.

Tip... You can buy prepared coriander or parsley in small
jars, ready for immediate use. Keep refrigerated once
opened, and use within six weeks.

Chargrilled chicken Caesar salad

Serves 2
276 calories per serving
Takes 15 minutes

This low-calorie version of a modern classic comes complete with a creamy dressing and crisp crunchy croûtons.

25 g (1 oz) white bread, without crusts, cut into 1 cm (½ inch) cubes

calorie controlled cooking spray

2 x 125 g (4½ oz) skinless, boneless chicken breasts

2 tablespoons extra light mayonnaise

2 tablespoons low fat natural yogurt

½ teaspoon Dijon mustard

1 teaspoon lemon juice

3 tablespoons skimmed milk

1 small Cos lettuce, shredded roughly

2 teaspoons freshly grated Parmesan cheese

4 anchovy fillets, chopped finely

salt and freshly ground black pepper

1 Preheat the oven to Gas Mark 4/180°C/fan oven 160°C. Spread out the cubed bread on a baking tray and lightly coat with cooking spray. Bake for 6–7 minutes until golden brown and crisp.

2 Meanwhile, preheat a griddle pan or non-stick frying pan on the hob. Cut each chicken breast in half horizontally to give two thin slices. Season and spray with cooking spray, then cook for 3–4 minutes each side or until cooked through.

3 To make the dressing, whisk the mayonnaise, yogurt, mustard and lemon juice together with some seasoning and then gradually blend in the milk.

4 Toss the shredded lettuce with half of the dressing then divide between two plates or bowls. Scatter the Parmesan, anchovies and croutons over the salads then top with the cooked chicken, sliced into thin strips, and drizzle with the remaining dressing. Serve immediately.

Tip… You can make double the quantity of croûtons and store them in an airtight container to keep them crisp – they make a great low calorie garnish for a bowl of soup.

Variation… If you like garlic croûtons, rub the bread with ½ garlic clove before cutting it into cubes.

Crunchy chicken salad

Serves 2
280 calories per serving
Takes 10 minutes

A modern take on a traditional Waldorf salad – with a creamy dressing and crisp pitta-bread croûtons.

1 Heat a non-stick frying pan. Spray the pitta bread pieces with the cooking spray and fry until golden and crisp.

2 Meanwhile, toss the apple slices in 1 teaspoon of the lemon juice. Place the lettuce, cabbage, celery, apple and pitta bread on a serving dish and arrange the cooked chicken on top.

3 Mix together the ingredients for the dressing with the remaining lemon juice and season to taste. Drizzle over the salad and serve immediately.

1 pitta bread, split open and torn into bite size pieces
calorie controlled cooking spray
1 small apple, quartered and cored and sliced thinly
juice of ¼ a lemon
100 g (3½ oz) Little Gem lettuce, leaves shredded
50 g (1¾ oz) red cabbage, chopped finely
1 celery stick, sliced finely
150 g (5½ oz) cooked, skinless chicken, cut into large chunks

For the dressing
2 tablespoons extra light mayonnaise
½ teaspoon extra virgin olive oil
1 small garlic clove, crushed
2 tablespoons 0% fat Greek yogurt
salt and freshly ground black pepper

Fruity chicken and rice salad

Serves 4

324 calories per serving

Takes 15 minutes to prepare,
20 minutes to cook

200 g (7 oz) long grain rice

**1 vegetable stock cube,
crumbled**

**225 g (8 oz) cooked, skinless
chicken breast, chopped**

**227 g can pineapple pieces in
natural juice, drained**

**150 g (5½ oz) red and green
seedless grapes, halved**

25 g (1 oz) sultanas or raisins

**50 g (1¾ oz) ready to eat,
semi-dried apricots,
chopped**

a squeeze of lemon juice

**a few mint leaves, torn into
pieces (optional)**

freshly ground black pepper

*A refreshing summer lunch that also makes a great buffet
salad.*

1 Bring a pan of water to the boil, add the rice with the
crumbled stock cube and cook according to the packet
instructions until tender. Drain, rinse with cold water to cool
quickly, then drain thoroughly.

2 Tip the rice into a large serving bowl and add the chicken,
and all of the fruit, then squeeze in the lemon juice. Add the
mint leaves, if using, then stir gently to mix all the ingredients
together. Season with black pepper. Share between four plates
or bowls and serve at once.

Tip... Keep any leftovers in a covered container in the
fridge and use within two days.

Oriental chicken noodle salad

Serves 2
416 calories per serving
Takes 35 minutes

100 g (3½ oz) dried
  wholewheat noodles
1 teaspoon sesame seeds
300 g (10½ oz) skinless,
  boneless chicken breasts,
  cut into bite size pieces
calorie controlled cooking
  spray
50 g (1¾ oz) baby spinach
  leaves, long stalks discarded
75 g (2¾ oz) radishes,
  trimmed and sliced
2 spring onions, sliced
5 cm (2 inches) cucumber,
  quartered, de-seeded and
  cut into thin strips
a few fresh basil leaves

For the dressing
1 cm (½ inch) fresh root
  ginger, peeled and grated
1 tablespoon balsamic vinegar
1 tablespoon light soy sauce
2 tablespoons orange juice
½ teaspoon toasted sesame
  oil
a pinch of dried chilli flakes

*Fresh and vibrant, this substantial salad has a piquant
ginger, soy and orange dressing. The chilli is optional but
it does give it a warming lift.*

1 Bring a pan of water to the boil and cook the noodles
according to the packet instructions, then drain and refresh
under cold running water. Place in a bowl, cover with cold
water, and set aside.

2 Heat a large wok or non-stick frying pan and dry fry the
sesame seeds for about 3 minutes, turning occasionally, until
golden. Remove from the pan and set aside.

3 Spray the chicken pieces with the cooking spray and place
in the hot wok or frying pan. Stir-fry for 6–8 minutes until
cooked and golden all over.

4 Meanwhile, make the dressing. Squeeze the ginger, using
your hands, and mix the juice with the rest of the dressing
ingredients. Discard the remaining fibrous bits of ginger.
Drain the noodles, return to the bowl and then combine
with the spinach, radishes, spring onions and cucumber.
Spoon over the dressing, toss together and then divide
between two large shallow bowls or plates. Top with the
chicken, basil leaves and sesame seeds. Serve while the
chicken is hot or leave it to cool if you prefer.

☮ **Variation…** Replace the chicken with 200 g (7 oz) Quorn
pieces. Add them in step 3 and stir-fry for about 3 minutes
until slightly golden.

Tangy chicken and avocado salad

Serves 1
310 calories per serving
Takes 8 minutes

**grated zest and juice of ½ a
  lime**
**2 tablespoons low fat natural
  yogurt**
**½ a ripe medium avocado,
  sliced**
**4 Romaine lettuce leaves,
  rinsed and shredded**
**75 g (2¾ oz) cherry tomatoes,
  quartered**
**100 g (3½ oz) cooked, skinless
  chicken breast, sliced**
**salt and freshly ground black
  pepper**

*Treat yourself to a proper lunch for one. The lime and
yogurt dressing gives this salad a really refreshing flavour.*

1 Mix the lime zest and half the juice with the yogurt and
seasoning to make a tangy dressing.

2 Toss the sliced avocado with the remaining lime juice.

3 Make a bed of shredded lettuce in a bowl then add the
cherry tomatoes, avocado and sliced chicken. Drizzle on the
dressing just before serving.

Sunshine chicken salad

Serves 4
240 calories per serving
Takes 15 minutes

2 tablespoons lime or lemon juice

125 g (4½ oz) red or green seedless grapes, halved

10 cm (4 inch) piece of cucumber, chopped

450 g (1 lb) cooked, skinless chicken, cut into strips

packet of mixed lettuce leaves

1 red pepper, de-seeded and sliced

1 yellow pepper, de-seeded and sliced

2 teaspoons sesame seeds, toasted (see Tip)

salt and freshly ground black pepper

For the dressing

150 g (5½ oz) low fat natural yogurt

1 teaspoon ground cumin

1 tablespoon chopped fresh mint

Make this tasty recipe with ready-cooked chicken from the supermarket or use up any leftovers from a roast.

1 Put the lime or lemon juice into a large serving bowl and add the grapes and cucumber, tossing to coat. Add the chicken and season with a little salt and black pepper.

2 To make the dressing, combine the yogurt, cumin and mint, and season. Chill the salad and dressing separately until ready to serve.

3 Pile the mixed lettuce leaves and peppers on to four plates, then divide the chicken mixture between them. Drizzle with the dressing, sprinkle with toasted sesame seeds and serve at once.

Tip… To toast sesame seeds, heat a small frying pan without fat, add the seeds and heat, stirring often, until lightly browned.

Artichoke and chicken salad

Serves 1
201 calories per serving
Takes 10 minutes

50 g (1¾ oz) cooked, skinless chicken, shredded

25 g (1 oz) low fat soft cheese with garlic and herbs

25 g (1 oz) 0% fat Greek yogurt

1 teaspoon wholegrain mustard

1 tablespoon chopped fresh flat leaf parsley

½ x 400 g can artichoke hearts in brine, drained and quartered

25 g (1 oz) mild or hot pepperdew peppers from a jar, drained and sliced

60 g (2 oz) cucumber, cubed

¼ x 137 g bag spinach, watercress and rocket salad

salt and freshly ground black pepper

Turn leftover roast chicken into a sophisticated Mediterranean-style salad.

1 In a bowl, mix together the chicken, soft cheese, yogurt, mustard and parsley and season. Gently fold through the artichoke hearts, peppers and cucumber.

2 Put the salad leaves on to a plate and top with the creamy chicken mixture. Serve immediately.

Sweet potato and chicken salad

Serves 2
208 calories per serving
Takes 15 minutes

200 g (7 oz) sweet potatoes, peeled and cut into 1 cm (½ inch) cubes
1 celery stick, sliced finely
2.5 cm (1 inch) cucumber, quartered, de-seeded and sliced
100 g (3½ oz) cooked, skinless chicken breast, cubed
¼ red onion, cubed
2 sprigs of fresh mint
1 Little Gem lettuce, shredded

For the dressing
2 tablespoons low fat natural yogurt
1 tablespoon extra light mayonnaise
1 tablespoon smooth mango chutney
1 teaspoon curry powder
1 tablespoon lemon juice
¼ teaspoon dried chilli flakes
salt and freshly ground black pepper

This lightly spiced salad is ideal for a quick and delicious lunch.

1 Bring a saucepan of water to the boil, add the sweet potatoes and cook for about 10 minutes or until tender. Drain, set aside and leave to cool.

2 To make the dressing, mix together all the ingredients with 1 tablespoon of water in a small bowl. Season to taste.

3 Put the sweet potatoes, celery, cucumber, chicken and red onion in a serving bowl, spoon the dressing over and toss the salad until coated. Scatter the mint leaves over before serving on a bed of shredded lettuce.

🍲 **Variation…** Replace the chicken with 100 g (3½ oz) Quorn Chicken Style Pieces. To prepare, spray with cooking spray and stir-fry for 8–10 minutes. Leave to cool before adding to the salad in step 3.

Teriyaki chicken salad

Serves 4
185 calories per serving
Takes 25 minutes + 30
   minutes marinating

1 teaspoon groundnut oil
3 tablespoons soy sauce
1 garlic clove, crushed
2 tablespoons sherry
grated zest and segments of
   an orange
4 spring onions, sliced
3 x 165 g (5¾ oz) skinless,
   boneless chicken breasts,
   cut into strips
100 g (3½ oz) pak choi
50 g (1¾ oz) beansprouts

*This tangy salad is an ideal starter for a dinner party – it
will certainly wake up your taste buds.*

1 Mix together the groundnut oil, soy sauce, garlic, sherry,
orange zest and the spring onions in a dish to make a
marinade. Add the chicken, cover with cling film and leave
in the fridge for 30 minutes.

2 Heat a griddle or wok and with a slotted spoon, transfer
the chicken pieces to it. Reserve the marinade.Cook for
6–8 minutes, turning often, until the chicken is cooked
through. Pour over the remaining marinade and cook for
1 or 2 minutes.

3 Divide the pak choi, orange segments and beansprouts
between four plates or shallow bowls and pour over the
chicken pieces and juices. Serve immediately.

Tip… Always make sure you heat the griddle or wok to
a high temperature before you start cooking.

Variation… For a more substantial meal, cook 60 g (2 oz)
of egg noodles per person to serve with this dish.

Snacks and light bites

Chicken and vegetable samosas

Makes 15

111 calories per samosa

Takes 35 minutes to prepare,
25 minutes to cook

100 g (3½ oz) floury potatoes,
such as Maris Piper, peeled
and quartered

50 g (1¾ oz) frozen petits pois

175 g (6 oz) skinless, boneless
chicken breast, cut into bite
size pieces

calorie controlled cooking
spray

1 small onion, chopped finely

1 small carrot, chopped finely

1 cm (½ inch) fresh root
ginger, peeled and chopped

1 teaspoon garam masala

½ teaspoon chilli powder

½ teaspoon cumin powder

1 tablespoon lemon juice

2 tablespoons chopped fresh
coriander, plus extra to
garnish

9 x 45 g (1½ oz) sheets filo
pastry, measuring 50 x
24 cm (20 x 9½ inches),
defrosted if frozen

salt and freshly ground black
pepper

mango chutney, to serve

*Baking samosas rather than frying them keeps the calorie
count way down.*

1 Bring a pan of water to the boil, add the potatoes and cook
for about 10 minutes or until tender. Add the peas 2 minutes
before the end of the cooking time. Drain and set aside.

2 Meanwhile, heat a wok or non stick frying pan until hot.
Spray the chicken with the cooking spray and stir-fry for 6–8
minutes until golden and cooked through. Remove from the
pan and set aside. Add the onion, carrot and ginger. Spray
the vegetables with the cooking spray. Stir-fry for 5 minutes,
adding a splash of water if they start to stick. Stir in the spices
and then transfer the mixture to a mixing bowl.

3 Cut the potatoes and chicken into cubes and add to the bowl
with the vegetables, plus lemon juice, coriander and seasoning.

4 Preheat the oven to Gas Mark 6/200°C/fan oven 180°C. Take
three sheets of filo and place one on top of the other (keep the
remaining filo covered). Using a cutter or bowl as a template,
cut out 5 x 13 cm (5 inch) rounds. Spray each round with the
cooking spray and then stack all 3 rounds on top of each other
again. Place a heaped tablespoonful of the chicken mixture on
one quarter of the filo round, wet the edge with water, then fold
the pastry over to make a semi-circle. Fold over again to make
a triangle and pinch to seal. Repeat to make 15 samosas.

5 Spray two large baking trays with the cooking spray, place
the samosas on the trays and spray again. Bake for 25 minutes
until light golden. Serve warm, garnished with coriander, and
with mango chutney on the side.

Chicken and shallot kebabs

Serves 2
195 calories per serving
Takes 20 minutes to prepare,
  15 minutes to cook

**225 g (8 oz) skinless, boneless
  chicken breasts, cubed**
1 teaspoon clear honey
**2 tablespoons chopped fresh
  mint**
½ teaspoon dried oregano
**finely grated zest and juice of
  ½ a lemon**
a pinch of salt
**1 garlic clove, chopped very
  finely**
2 teaspoons olive oil
8 shallots
4 bay leaves
freshly ground black pepper

To serve
fresh salad leaves
lemon wedges

*These tasty kebabs, with a hint of exotic Greek flavours,
are delicious served hot or cold.*

1 Place the chicken in a dish with the honey, mint, oregano,
lemon zest and juice, salt, garlic, olive oil and black pepper.
Mix together well.

2 Preheat the grill to medium. Thread the chicken pieces and
shallots on to four skewers – allow two shallots per skewer,
and thread a bay leaf half way through.

3 Grill the kebabs for 10–15 minutes, turning frequently, until
the chicken is golden and cooked through.

4 Serve two kebabs per person on a bed of mixed salad
leaves, garnished with a lemon wedge.

Tips… If you prefer the shallots with a softer texture, place
them in a small saucepan of water and bring to the boil.
Reduce the heat, cover and simmer for 5 minutes before
threading them on the skewers.

When using wooden skewers, soak them first in cold water
for 30 minutes, to stop them from burning under the grill or
on the barbecue.

Chicken pot noodle

Serves 2
420 calories per serving
Takes 15 minutes

700 ml (1¼ pints) chicken
  stock
1½ teaspoons Madras curry
  paste
115 g (4¼ oz) dried medium
  egg noodles
750 g (1 lb 10 oz) frozen mixed
  vegetables such as green
  beans, broccoli, cauliflower
  and carrots
100 g (3½ oz) skinless,
  boneless chicken breast,
  sliced then cut into thin
  strips
4 tablespoons chopped fresh
  coriander
4 spring onions, shredded

*If you want something quick and filling, try this healthy
storecupboard version of a fast-food snack.*

1 Pour the stock into a lidded pan and add the curry paste.
Bring to the boil then add the noodles and frozen vegetables.
Cover and cook for 5 minutes.

2 Add the chicken, coriander and spring onions and cook for
a minute or two more (the chicken will cook quickly on impact
with the heat). Serve in bowls.

Variation... If you have any leftover chicken from a roast,
this recipe is a great way of using it up. Remove all traces
of skin first and add the cooked meat in step 2.

Chicken satay

Serves 1

260 calories per serving

Takes 25 minutes + at least
  15 minutes marinating

❄

**165 g (5¾ oz) skinless,
  boneless chicken breast,
  sliced into 4 long strips**

**lime wedges and shredded
  spring onions, to garnish**

For the marinade

1 garlic clove, crushed

**2.5 cm (1 inch) piece of fresh
  root ginger, peeled and
  grated finely**

1 tablespoon soy sauce

1 teaspoon clear honey

grated zest and juice of a lime

For the peanut sauce

**1 teaspoon crunchy peanut
  butter**

**1 tablespoon reduced fat
  coconut milk**

**salt and freshly ground black
  pepper**

1 Mix together the marinade ingredients in a bowl and add the chicken strips. Toss together, coating the chicken, then leave in the fridge for at least 15 minutes or overnight.

2 Preheat the grill to high, drain the marinade into a small saucepan and thread one strip of chicken on to each skewer (see Tip on page 46). Grill for 3 minutes on each side, until golden brown and cooked through, brushing every now and then with the marinade.

3 Bring the remaining marinade to the boil for a minute or so and then add the peanut sauce ingredients and a tablespoon of water if the sauce is too thick. Stir together until well blended and heated through. Serve the satay skewers with the peanut sauce for dipping.

Coleslaw with chicken and grapes

Serves 4
135 calories per serving
Takes 15 minutes

100 g (3½ oz) low fat soft
cheese

1 teaspoon Dijon mustard

6 tablespoons low fat natural
yogurt

2 teaspoons lemon juice

200 g (7 oz) white cabbage,
shredded finely

100 g (3½ oz) carrot, grated

¼ red onion, cubed finely

100 g (3½ oz) cooked,
skinless chicken (smoked if
available), sliced

200 g (7 oz) red or black
seedless grapes, halved

2 Romaine lettuce hearts,
shredded

salt and freshly ground black
pepper

1 tablespoon chopped fresh
flat leaf parsley, to garnish
(optional)

*A crunchy satisfying salad in a creamy dressing with a
hint of mustard.*

1 Beat the soft cheese, mustard, yogurt and lemon juice
together in a small bowl or jug. (A mini whisk is very useful
to get a smooth consistency.)

2 Place the cabbage, carrot, onion, chicken and grapes in
a large mixing bowl and add the soft cheese mixture. Mix
thoroughly and season to taste.

3 You can serve the coleslaw immediately, or it will keep for
at least 12 hours in a fridge. When ready to serve, place a bed
of shredded lettuce in four shallow bowls and put a quarter of
the coleslaw on each one. Garnish with the parsley, if using.

Chicken burgers

Serves 2
330 calories per serving
Takes 25 minutes
❄ (burgers only)

For the burgers
225 g (8 oz) chicken mince
½ small red onion, chopped finely
1 egg, beaten
25 g (1 oz) fresh wholemeal breadcrumbs
1 teaspoon dried mixed herbs

To serve
2 burger buns
1 tablespoon extra light mayonnaise
1 Little Gem lettuce, shredded
1 tomato, sliced

Try these delicious chicken burgers when you feel like a change from the classic beefburger.

1 Preheat the grill to high. Place all the burger ingredients in a bowl and mix well. Shape the mixture into two round flat burgers with your hands.

2 Cook the burgers under the grill for 5 minutes on each side.

3 Split each burger bun in half and toast them lightly. Spread one half of each with a little mayonnaise and top with lettuce and tomato. Place a burger and the remaining half bun on top of each. Serve at once.

Chilli crispy goujons

Serves 2
269 calories per serving
Takes 15 minutes

350 g (12 oz) skinless,
  boneless chicken breasts,
  cut into thin strips
2 teaspoons cornflour
2 tablespoons soy sauce
calorie controlled cooking
  spray
3 tablespoons sweet chilli
  sauce
½ teaspoon Thai fish sauce
2 fresh mint sprigs
½ x 25 g packet fresh
  coriander, leaves only
a lime, halved, to serve

You can put these Chinese-style chicken goujons on the table faster than fetching a take-away – and they'll be much lower in calories.

1 Mix together the chicken strips and cornflour in a bowl. Add the soy sauce and continue to mix until coated.

2 Heat a non-stick frying pan until hot and spray with the cooking spray. Add the chicken, and cook for 5–6 minutes, turning until brown all over. You may have to do this in batches.

3 Meanwhile, mix together the chilli sauce, 2 tablespoons of cold water and the fish sauce. Return all the chicken to the pan, pour the sauce over the chicken and cook for a further 2 minutes until cooked and starting to caramelise. Toss through the mint and coriander leaves and serve immediately with the lime halves.

Tip... Serve with 150 g (5½ oz) cooked brown rice per person and a mixed salad.

Lemony chicken lunch box

Serves 1
246 calories per serving
Takes 15 minutes

40 g (1½ oz) small pasta
   shapes, such as tubetti
grated zest of ½ a lemon
2 tablespoons low fat fromage
   frais
75 g (2¾ oz) roasted, skinless
   chicken breast, sliced
4 cherry tomatoes, halved
salt and freshly ground black
   pepper
rocket leaves, to serve

Enjoy this at your desk or for a picnic.

1 Bring a large pan of water to the boil and cook the pasta according to the packet instructions. Drain and rinse in cold water.

2 Mix together the lemon zest and fromage frais and season. Stir in the pasta, chicken and tomatoes and serve with a few rocket leaves.

Lime and coriander chicken bagel

Serves 1
326 calories per serving
Takes 5 minutes

1 plain bagel, halved
30 g (1¼ oz) low fat soft cheese
finely grated zest of ½ a lime
1 tablespoon chopped fresh coriander
60 g (2 oz) cooked, skinless chicken, sliced
15 g (½ oz) baby salad leaves
freshly ground black pepper

If you want to use up a little leftover roast chicken, this appetising bagel is a great way to do it.

1 Preheat the grill to a medium heat and lightly toast the bagel on the cut sides.

2 Mix the soft cheese with the lime zest, coriander and black pepper. Spread on both halves of the toasted bagel.

3 Pile the chicken and salad leaves on to the bottom half of the bagel and top with the other half to serve.

Tip… When you buy a packet of bagels, slice the fresh bagels in half and freeze them. The bagel halves can then be toasted from frozen, so they're ready in an instant whenever you want them.

Jubilee chicken sandwich

Serves 2
315 calories per serving
Takes 10 minutes

4 medium slices wholemeal
  bread
2 teaspoons low fat spread
2 tablespoons low fat natural
  yogurt
¼ teaspoon medium curry
  powder
2 teaspoons chopped fresh
  coriander (optional)
100 g (3½ oz) skinless, cooked
  chicken breast, sliced
2 crisp lettuce leaves,
  shredded
¼ small red onion or 1 spring
  onion, sliced thinly
75 g (2¾ oz) roasted red
  peppers in brine, sliced
salt and freshly ground black
  pepper

A hint of curry gives this delicious sandwich a tasty kick.

1 Spread each slice of bread with the low fat spread.

2 Mix together the yogurt and curry powder, then stir in the coriander, if using. Add the chicken slices, tossing to coat in the mixture.

3 Share the lettuce between two slices of bread, then arrange the chicken on top. Sprinkle with the onion then divide the red pepper between them.

4 Season, sandwich together with the remaining bread, then cut in half. Serve at once, or wrap in cling film and keep chilled to eat later.

Tip... Make sure you don't add too much curry powder. If you prefer a milder flavour, simply add a generous pinch, or use a mild curry powder instead.

Roast chicken 'roll up'

Serves 1
114 calories per serving
Takes 5 minutes

2 teaspoons low fat soft cheese
1 teaspoon lemon juice
1 spring onion, chopped finely
75 g (2¾ oz) roast chicken (approx 2 slices)
4 strips of red pepper
freshly ground black pepper

A speedy snack for when you're feeling peckish, this chicken 'roll up' would also be ideal for a lunchbox. Serve with sticks of carrot and celery.

1 In a bowl, mix together the soft cheese, lemon juice and spring onion.

2 Spoon the soft cheese mixture down one side of each chicken slice, season with black pepper and then top each with two strips of red pepper. Roll up the chicken slices to encase the filling and wrap in cling film until ready to eat.

Variations... Instead of roast chicken, use the same weight of roast beef. Stir ½ teaspoon of horseradish sauce into the soft cheese mixture. Or try it with the same weight of roast pork and replace the red pepper with thin slices of apple.

Seared chicken with mint yogurt dressing

Serves 2
379 calories per serving
Takes 25 minutes

75 g (2¾ oz) dried wholewheat couscous

½ teaspoon vegetable stock powder or ½ a stock cube

300 g (10½ oz) skinless, boneless chicken breast, cut into 1 cm (½ inch) wide strips

2 teaspoons dried thyme

2 teaspoons ground coriander

calorie controlled cooking spray

50 g (1¾ oz) frozen peas

50 g (1¾ oz) sugar snap peas, sliced diagonally

½ red pepper, de-seeded and cut into thin strips

1 spring onion, sliced diagonally

salt and freshly ground black pepper

For the mint yogurt dressing
a small handful of fresh mint leaves

75 g (2¾ oz) 0% fat Greek yogurt

juice of ½ a lime

½ teaspoon cumin seeds

Using a griddle pan gives the chicken those appetising char-grill stripes.

1 Put the couscous in a bowl, pour over enough boiling water to cover, stir in the stock powder or crumble in the cube and cover with a plate. Leave for about 5 minutes or until the stock is absorbed and the grains are tender. Using a fork, fluff up the couscous and set aside.

2 Meanwhile, using a hand held blender, blend together all the dressing ingredients, except the cumin seeds. If you don't have a hand held blender, finely chop the mint and combine with the remaining ingredients. Transfer to a bowl, season and scatter over the cumin seeds.

3 Sprinkle the chicken with the thyme, coriander and seasoning. Turn the strips until evenly coated. Heat a griddle pan or non-stick frying pan over a high heat. Spray the chicken with the cooking spray. Cook over a medium-high heat for 6 minutes, turning once, until cooked through and golden.

4 Meanwhile, bring a saucepan of water to the boil, add the peas, sugar snap peas, pepper and spring onion and cook for 3 minutes or until tender. Drain and refresh under cold water.

5 To serve, divide the couscous between two large, shallow bowls then top with the peas, sugar snap peas, red pepper, spring onion and chicken. Spoon over the dressing.

Ⓥ Variation... Swap the chicken for 2 x 15 g (½ oz) slices of light halloumi per person. Pat the cheese dry with kitchen towel and prepare in the same way as the chicken in step 3, then griddle or pan-fry for 2 minutes on each side.

Sesame chicken parcels

Serves 2
283 calories per serving
Takes 25 minutes

½ teaspoon toasted sesame
oil
2 tablespoons teriyaki
marinade
1 tablespoon light soy sauce
2 x 150 g (5½ oz) skinless,
boneless chicken breasts
1 cm (½ inch) fresh root
ginger, peeled and sliced
into rounds
2 spring onions, shredded
½ teaspoon sesame seeds
2 carrots, cut into ribbons
using a vegetable peeler
2 teaspoons lime juice, plus
lime slices, to garnish

For the wasabi dip
4 teaspoons extra light
mayonnaise
2 teaspoons wasabi paste

Cooking the chicken in a parcel helps to keep it moist and succulent; it's a great way to cook fish, too.

1 Preheat the oven to Gas Mark 6/200°C/fan oven 180°C. Mix together the sesame oil, teriyaki marinade and soy sauce.

2 Place each chicken breast on a piece of foil, large enough to make a parcel. Spoon over the teriyaki mixture then arrange the ginger and spring onions on top. Fold over the foil and seal to make two loose parcels then place on a baking sheet.

3 Bake in the oven for 20 minutes until the chicken is cooked through and there is no trace of pink in the centre.

4 While the chicken is cooking, dry fry the sesame seeds by putting them in a dry non-stick frying pan over a medium heat, shaking the pan occasionally, for about 3 minutes until lightly golden. Mix together the ingredients for the wasabi dip with 1 teaspoon of warm water.

5 Carefully open each parcel on to a plate. Arrange the carrots by the side, squeeze over the lime juice and sprinkle with the sesame seeds. Serve with a spoonful of the wasabi dip.

Smoked chicken skewers

Serves 2
170 calories per serving
Takes 18 minutes

½ teaspoon cayenne pepper

½ teaspoon ground cumin

½ teaspoon smoked paprika (see Tip)

a generous pinch of mild or hot chilli powder

300 g (10½ oz) skinless, boneless chicken breasts, cut into thin strips

1 small courgette, trimmed and cut into ribbons using a vegetable peeler

calorie controlled cooking spray

salt and freshly ground black pepper

Cook these kebabs under the grill or on the barbecue if the weather is nice.

1 Mix the cayenne pepper, cumin, paprika, chilli powder and seasoning together in a bowl. Add the chicken strips and toss them in the spices until coated. Set aside.

2 Thread a strip of chicken on to a skewer (see Tip on page 46) then fold up a few courgette slices concertina-style and thread them on to the skewer. Repeat with the remaining chicken and courgette slices to make a total of six skewers.

3 Preheat the grill to medium high. Put the skewers on a grill pan and spray with the cooking spray. Cook the skewers under the grill for 10 minutes, turning until golden and cooked through. Serve immediately.

Tip... Smoked paprika is available in most large supermarkets next to the other dried herbs and spices but if you can't find it, you can use normal paprika instead.

Variation... Serve with a medium pitta, salad leaves, sliced tomatoes and 1 tablespoon of tzatziki per person.

For family and friends

Open-crust chicken and mushroom pie

Serves 6

220 calories per serving

Takes 35 minutes to prepare +
30 minutes chilling,
50–55 minutes to cook

For the pastry

**110 g (4 oz) plain flour, plus
2 tablespoons for rolling**

a pinch of salt

60 g (2 oz) low fat spread

For the filling

1 teaspoon sunflower oil

**175 g (6 oz) skinless, boneless
chicken breast, cubed**

1 onion, chopped

1 garlic clove, crushed

**110 g (4 oz) closed-cup
mushrooms, sliced**

4 tomatoes, peeled and chopped

2 tablespoons tomato purée

1 large courgette, chopped

**1 tablespoon chopped fresh
tarragon, or 1 teaspoon dried**

1 egg, separated

15 g (½ oz) semolina

**1 teaspoon grated Parmesan
cheese**

**salt and freshly ground black
pepper**

This rustic open-crust pie is delicious hot or cold.

1 To make the pastry, sift the flour and salt into a large bowl then lightly rub in the margarine until the mixture resembles fine breadcrumbs. Using a blunt-ended knife, stir in enough ice cold water – about 3 or 4 tablespoons – to form a soft, but not sticky, dough. Knead the dough lightly until smooth. Place it in a polythene bag then chill for 30 minutes in the fridge.

2 To make the filling, heat the oil in a medium non-stick frying pan and cook the chicken, onion and garlic for 5 minutes over a medium heat. Add the mushrooms, tomatoes, tomato purée, courgette, tarragon and seasoning, and simmer gently for 15 minutes.

3 Preheat the oven to Gas Mark 6/200°C/fan oven 180°C. Roll out the chilled pastry on a lightly floured surface to form a rough 25 cm (10 inch) circle. Place it on a floured baking sheet.

4 Brush the pastry with egg yolk and sprinkle with the semolina. Spoon over the chicken and mushroom filling, leaving a 4 cm (1½ inch) border all around. Turn the edges of the pastry in to cover part of the filling.

5 Brush the folded-over pastry with egg white then sprinkle with the Parmesan. Bake the pie for 30–35 minutes, until golden.

🟡 **Variation…** For a vegetarian alternative, replace the chicken with Quorn.

Chicken casserole

Serves 4
240 calories per serving
Takes 15 minutes to prepare,
   1 hour to cook
❄

1 tablespoon vegetable oil
2 large onions, sliced
3 celery sticks, sliced
2 carrots, chopped
1 large leek, chopped
450 g (1 lb) skinless, boneless
   chicken breasts, cut into
   large chunks
150 ml (¼ pint) dry white wine
300 ml (½ pint) chicken stock
2 teaspoons dried mixed herbs
1 tablespoon cornflour
salt and freshly ground black
   pepper

*What could be more welcoming for family or friends than
a delicious chicken casserole?*

1 Preheat the oven to Gas Mark 4/180°C/fan oven 160°C.
Heat the vegetable oil in a large flameproof casserole, and
sauté the onions, celery, carrots and leek for about 5 minutes,
until softened.

2 Add the chicken to the casserole and cook until sealed
on all sides. Add the wine and allow it to bubble up for a few
moments. Pour in the chicken stock and add the dried mixed
herbs. Season. Put the lid on the casserole dish and transfer
it to the middle shelf of the oven. Cook for 45 minutes.

3 Blend the cornflour with about 3 tablespoons of cold water
to make a smooth paste. Add it to the casserole, stirring it in
to mix well. Return the casserole to the oven to cook for a
further 5 minutes. Check the seasoning before serving on
warmed plates.

Variation… Omit the white wine if you prefer and use a
total of 450 ml (16 fl oz) of chicken stock instead.

Chicken in red wine

Serves 6

256 calories per serving

Takes 20 minutes to prepare,
1¼ hours to cook

**calorie controlled cooking
spray**

**6 x 125g (4½ oz) skinless,
boneless chicken breasts**

**1 smoked lean back bacon
rasher, chopped**

**12 shallots, left whole, or 1
large onion, chopped**

1 garlic clove, crushed

1 leek, sliced

**250 g (9 oz) mushrooms,
halved**

**450 g (1 lb) small carrots,
trimmed and halved**

350 ml (12 fl oz) red wine

**700 ml (1¼ pints) chicken
stock**

**1 teaspoon dried tarragon or
thyme**

2 bay leaves

**2 tablespoons chopped fresh
flat leaf parsley**

**salt and freshly ground black
pepper**

Serve this French-inspired dish for a lazy Sunday lunch.

1 Preheat the oven to Gas Mark 4/180°C/fan oven 160°C.
Heat a large, lidded, flameproof casserole dish on the hob
until hot. Spray with the cooking spray.

2 Add the chicken breasts, letting them sear and brown before
turning them over. Cook for 3–4 minutes until browned on both
sides. (Alternatively, brown the chicken in a non-stick frying
pan first, then transfer to a regular casserole dish).

3 Add the bacon, shallots or onion, garlic, leek, mushrooms
and carrots. Pour in the wine and stock, then add all the herbs.
Season and cover. Transfer to the oven and bake for 1–1¼
hours. Remove the bay leaves before serving.

Tip... Bake 6 medium jacket potatoes (225 g/8 oz each)
on the shelf above while the casserole cooks.

Chicken hotpot

Serves 4

400 calories per serving

Takes 15 minutes to prepare,
1 hour 30 minutes to cook

❄

4 skinless chicken legs, each
approximately 200 g (7oz)

25 g (1 oz) seasoned flour

1 tablespoon vegetable oil

2 large carrots, cut into 2 cm
(¾ inch) slices

3 sticks celery, sliced

125 g (4½ oz) green cabbage,
shredded

2 medium leeks, trimmed and
cut into 2 cm (¾ inch) slices

1 tablespoon chopped fresh
thyme

2 baking potatoes, each
approximately 300 g
(10½ oz), cut into 5 mm
(¼ inch) slices

425 ml (15 fl oz) hot chicken
or vegetable stock

2 teaspoons cornflour, blended
with a little cold water

salt and freshly ground black
pepper

*A warming chicken and vegetable dish topped with sliced
potatoes.*

1 Preheat the oven to Gas Mark 5/190°C/fan oven 170°C.
Lightly dust the chicken joints with the seasoned flour. Heat
the oil in a non-stick frying pan, and sauté the chicken for
3–4 minutes, or until lightly browned on all sides.

2 Put half of the carrots, celery, cabbage and leeks over the
base of a large casserole dish and season them. Top with
the chicken legs, scatter with the thyme and cover with the
remaining vegetables. Overlap the potato slices on top of the
vegetables.

3 Stir the hot stock into the blended cornflour until smooth
and gently pour it over the casserole. Cover the dish lightly
with a piece of foil, and cook in the oven for an hour.

4 Remove the foil, increase the oven temperature to
Gas Mark 6/ 200°C/fan oven 180°C, and cook for a further
25–30 minutes, until the potatoes are tender and golden.

Variations... Use 8 skinless, boneless chicken thighs
instead of the chicken legs.

For a lamb hotpot, replace the chicken with 4 x 125 g
(4½ oz) lean lamb loin chops. Add these at step 2, and
reduce the cooking time at step 3 to 30 minutes. Replace
the thyme with rosemary.

Chilled curried chicken

Serves 4

185 calories per serving

Takes 25 minutes to prepare, 20 minutes to cook + 1 hour chilling

❄

2 x 165 g (5¾ oz) skinless, boneless chicken breasts

½ tablespoon seasoned flour

calorie controlled cooking spray

2 onions, chopped

1 cooking apple, peeled, quartered and sliced

1 tablespoon mango chutney

1 tablespoon curry powder

1 teaspoon ground cinnamon

1 teaspoon ground ginger

150 ml (5 fl oz) skimmed milk

150 g (5½ oz) low fat natural yogurt

1–2 tablespoons chopped fresh coriander

salt and freshly ground black pepper

A delicately spiced dish with a fruity sauce.

1 Coat the chicken in the seasoned flour. Spray a large non-stick frying pan with the cooking spray and heat to a medium heat. Brown the chicken breasts on both sides and remove them from the pan.

2 Spray the pan with more cooking spray and add the onions. Stir them for a minute or two until starting to soften. Add the apple, chutney and spices. Cook for another couple of minutes, stirring all the time.

3 Add 150 ml (¼ pint) water and the milk. Bring up to simmering point and return the chicken to the pan. Simmer gently, uncovered, for 20 minutes or until the chicken is cooked through. Stir occasionally to prevent sticking.

4 Remove the pan from the heat. Put the chicken on a chopping board and spoon the sauce into a serving bowl. Cut the chicken into bite size pieces and stir back into the sauce. Add the yogurt and coriander. Season to taste and chill for at least 1 hour or overnight before serving.

Tip... Serve with warmed garlic and coriander naan bread.

Chicken with pesto roast vegetables

Serves 6
369 calories per serving
Takes 25 minutes to prepare,
1 hour 35 minutes to cook

1.4 kg (3 lb) chicken
1 large lemon
a few fresh herb sprigs, such as sage or basil
600 g (1 lb 5 oz) baby new potatoes, unpeeled and halved
2 large red onions, cut into wedges
1 garlic bulb, separated into unpeeled cloves
2 red peppers, de-seeded and quartered
400 ml (14 fl oz) hot chicken stock
1 tablespoon white wine vinegar
3 tablespoons green pesto
2 courgettes, sliced
390 g can artichoke hearts in water, drained and quartered
calorie controlled cooking spray
salt and freshly ground black pepper

Roast chicken is a real family favourite and this version is packed with flavour.

1 Preheat the oven to Gas Mark 4/180°C/fan oven 160°C. Remove all the visible fat from the chicken, especially inside the body cavity, and trim off any loose skin. Squeeze the juice from the lemon into a bowl and set aside. Put the shells of the lemon inside the body cavity with the sage or basil. Place in a very large roasting tin and season.

2 Scatter the potatoes, onions, garlic and peppers around the chicken. In a jug, stir the stock with the vinegar and 1 tablespoon of the pesto and pour over the chicken and vegetables. Cover with foil and roast for 1 hour.

3 Meanwhile, mix the lemon juice with the remaining pesto and 2 tablespoons of water.

4 Turn the oven up to Gas Mark 7/220°C/fan oven 200°C. Uncover the chicken and scatter the courgettes and artichoke hearts around the tin. Spray with cooking spray and spoon over the pesto and lemon mixture, then return to the oven for 35 minutes more until the chicken is cooked and the vegetables are tender.

5 Carve the chicken and serve, without skin, with the vegetables and juices, skimming off any visible fat.

Tip... Serve with steamed broccoli.

Chicken, ham and sweetcorn bake

Serves 4

475 calories per serving

Takes 25 minutes to prepare,
45 minutes to cook

❄

**750 g (1 lb 10 oz) potatoes,
chopped**

350 ml (12 fl oz) skimmed milk

25 g (1 oz) low fat spread

50 g (1¾ oz) plain flour

300 ml (10 fl oz) chicken stock

**350 g (12 oz) cooked, skinless
chicken, cut into chunks**

**50 g (1¾ oz) cooked ham,
chopped**

**100 g (3½ oz) canned or
frozen sweetcorn**

**1 tablespoon chopped fresh
parsley plus extra to garnish**

**salt and freshly ground black
pepper**

*Chicken, ham and sweetcorn, topped with sliced cooked
potatoes, makes a satisfying main course dish.*

1 Cook the potatoes in plenty of boiling water until just tender,
about 15 minutes. Mash well, adding 50 ml (2 fl oz) of milk,
and season with a little pepper.

2 Preheat the oven to Gas Mark 6/200°C/fan oven 180°C.
Grease a 2 litre (3½ pint) shallow ovenproof dish with
1 teaspoon of the margarine.

3 Melt the remaining margarine in a medium-sized saucepan.
Add the flour, stirring to blend. Cook gently for 1 minute, then
remove from the heat. Gradually blend in the remaining milk,
then stir in the chicken stock. Return to the heat, stirring
continuously until the sauce boils and thickens.

4 Add the chicken, ham, sweetcorn and parsley to the sauce.
Season with salt and pepper.

5 Pour the chicken and ham mixture into the baking dish and
top with the mashed potatoes. Bake for 25–30 minutes, or until
the potatoes are lightly browned. Serve sprinkled with the extra
chopped parsley.

Variation… Use cooked turkey instead of chicken, if you
prefer, and try chopped fresh tarragon instead of parsley.

Garlic and bacon chicken bake

Serves 4
347 calories per serving
Takes 50 minutes
❄

6 medium potatoes, chopped
100 g (3½ oz) lardons
1 tablespoon chopped fresh oregano
12 garlic cloves, unpeeled
calorie controlled cooking spray
4 x 165 g (5¾ oz) chicken breasts
salt and freshly ground black pepper

A dish for real garlic lovers. Serve with steamed green beans or mange tout.

1 Preheat the oven to Gas Mark 6/200°C/fan oven 180°C. Place the potatoes, bacon, oregano and garlic in a roasting tray. Season and spray with the cooking spray and toss to combine.

2 Bake for 15 minutes, toss gently, then return to the oven for another 10–15 minutes.

3 Meanwhile, season the chicken breasts. Spray a non-stick frying pan with the cooking spray and cook the chicken for 2–3 minutes on each side until slightly golden. Place the chicken on top of the potatoes and garlic and return to the oven for another 10 minutes, until the chicken is cooked through.

4 To serve, place the chicken and potatoes on the plates and squeeze the garlic from its skin on top.

Crispy garlic chicken breasts

Serves 4
246 calories per serving
Takes 15 minutes to prepare,
   20 minutes to cook

2 garlic cloves, crushed
1 tablespoon finely chopped fresh parsley
75 g (2¾ oz) low fat soft cheese
4 x 125 g (4½ oz) skinless, boneless chicken breasts
1 egg
1 tablespoon skimmed milk
75 g (2¾ oz) fresh white breadcrumbs
calorie controlled cooking spray
freshly ground black pepper

This is a delicious way to infuse chicken breasts with a hint of garlic – but without the high calorie count of traditional chicken Kiev.

1 Preheat the oven to Gas Mark 6/200°C/fan oven 180°C. In a bowl, mix the garlic and parsley with the soft cheese and black pepper. Cut a deep pocket in each chicken breast, taking care not to cut right through, then stuff the soft cheese mixture inside, closing the flesh around the stuffing as far as possible.

2 Beat the egg with the milk in a shallow dish, and spread the crumbs out on a plate. Dip each chicken breast first in the egg mixture and then in crumbs to coat all over. Place on a non-stick baking tray and spray with the cooking spray. Bake for 20 minutes until crisp and cooked through.

Tip… Serve with new potatoes and green vegetables.

Chicken cordon bleu

Serves 4

270 calories per serving

Takes 20 minutes to prepare,
35 minutes to cook

❄

**4 x 150 g (5½ oz) skinless,
boneless chicken breasts**

50 g (1¾ oz) wafer-thin ham

**50 g (1¾ oz) Gruyère or
Cheddar cheese, finely
grated**

1 small egg

**50 g (1¾ oz) dried
breadcrumbs**

**salt and freshly ground black
pepper**

lemon wedges, to serve

*Coating the chicken breasts in breadcrumbs before baking
keeps them beautifully moist.*

1 Preheat the oven to Gas Mark 5/190°C/fan oven 170°C.
Using a sharp knife, cut a pocket into each chicken breast.
Stuff each pocket with an equal amount of ham and cheese.
Season, then close the pockets and secure with cocktail sticks.

2 Beat the egg in a shallow dish with 2 tablespoons of cold
water. Sprinkle the breadcrumbs on to a plate. Dip each
chicken breast first into the egg, then into the breadcrumbs,
pressing them in well.

3 Arrange the chicken breasts in a roasting pan and cook for
30–35 minutes until tender. Test with a sharp knife: the juices
should run clear and there should be no traces of pink. Serve
with lemon wedges.

One-pot chicken

Serves 4

315 calories per serving

Takes 20 minutes to prepare,
50 minutes to cook

❄

1 tablespoon olive oil

4 x 125g (4½ oz) skinless,
boneless chicken breasts

12 shallots

3 carrots, chopped

2 leeks, sliced

1 tablespoon plain flour

1 chicken stock cube,
dissolved in 425 ml (15 fl oz)
hot water

100 ml (3½ fl oz) skimmed
milk

4 canned artichokes, drained
and halved

2 red peppers, de-seeded and
cut into thick strips

1 tablespoon wholegrain
mustard

salt and freshly ground black
pepper

*This wonderful one-pot chicken dish uses artichoke hearts
for a Spanish influence.*

1 Preheat the oven to Gas Mark 3/160°C/fan oven 140°C.
Heat half the olive oil in a non-stick frying pan, add the chicken
breasts and cook over a high heat for 1 minute, or until golden.
Turn them over and cook for another minute or so. Transfer the
chicken to a casserole dish.

2 Add the shallots to the frying pan and stir-fry them for 1–2
minutes, or until light golden brown, then transfer them to the
casserole. Add the carrots and leeks to the casserole dish.

3 Heat the remaining oil in the frying pan and add the flour,
stirring with a wooden spoon. Cook over a medium heat for
1 minute, stirring, then gradually add the stock, stirring as you
go. When all the stock has been incorporated, stir in the milk
and season.

4 Pour the sauce over the chicken and vegetables. Cover
with a lid or a piece of foil and transfer to the oven to cook
for 30 minutes.

5 Add the artichokes and red peppers to the casserole. Cook
for a further 15 minutes, or until the vegetables are tender. Just
before serving, stir in the wholegrain mustard.

Tip… Serve with spinach or green beans and boiled new
potatoes.

Variation… Add a chopped red or green fresh chilli if you
like a bit of heat.

Lemon and garlic roast chicken

Serves 4
255 calories per serving
Takes 20 minutes to prepare,
   1 hour to cook

1.5 kg (3 lb 5 oz) chicken
calorie controlled cooking
   spray
2 lemons
1 garlic bulb
300 ml (10 fl oz) chicken stock
salt and freshly ground black
   pepper

*A very easy recipe with a Mediterranean flavour, to enjoy
as a Sunday roast or evening dinner.*

1 Preheat the oven to Gas Mark 6/200°C/180°C. Place the
chicken in a roasting tin and spray with the cooking spray.
Season well both inside the cavity and all over the skin. Cut
each lemon in half and squeeze the juice over the skin of the
chicken and then place the squeezed shell inside the cavity.
Break off the garlic cloves from the bulb but do not remove
the skin. Put about 4 cloves inside the cavity of the chicken
and scatter the others in the roasting tin.

2 Roast for about 1 hour until cooked, basting frequently with
the juices in the tin. To test that it is ready, pierce the chicken
with a sharp knife or skewer; the juices should run clear.

3 When cooked, remove the chicken to a carving board,
tipping it up to leave behind any juices in the roasting tin.
Cover the chicken with foil and allow to rest for a few minutes
while you make the gravy.

4 To make the gravy, drain off any excess oil in the roasting
tin then put the tin on the hob. Squash the cooked garlic cloves
with a fork until they split; discard the skins and add the flesh
to the roasting tin. Heat the tin and add the chicken stock.
Use a wooden spoon or spatula to scrape up any bits stuck to
the tin, then boil rapidly for a few minutes until reduced a little.
Strain into a jug and serve with the carved meat.

Roast chicken ratatouille

Serves 4
216 calories per serving
Takes 10 minutes to prepare,
  30 minutes to cook

3 mixed peppers, de-seeded
  and chopped roughly
1 courgette, chopped roughly
1 aubergine, chopped roughly
2 garlic cloves, crushed
1 teaspoon dried mixed herbs,
  plus an extra pinch
calorie controlled cooking
  spray
4 x 150 g (5½ oz) skinless,
  boneless chicken breasts
400 g can chopped tomatoes

This Mediterranean-style roast is all baked in one tray so is really easy to make.

1 Preheat the oven to Gas Mark 6/200°C/fan oven 180°C. In a large roasting tin, toss together the peppers, courgette and aubergine with the garlic. Add 1 teaspoon of herbs and coat with cooking spray. Spread the vegetables out in a shallow layer, then put them in the oven for 15 minutes.

2 After 15 minutes, stir the vegetables around and push to one side of the tin. Sprinkle the chicken breasts with the pinch of dried mixed herbs and place in the space in the roasting tin. Return to the oven for 15 minutes.

3 Finally, mix the chopped tomatoes with the roasted vegetables and return to the oven for 5 minutes. Serve the chicken on top of the ratatouille.

Variation... For a vegetarian version, use 8 x 55 g (1¾ oz) Quorn Chicken Style Fillets instead of the chicken breasts.

Tip... Serve with a 225 g (8 oz) jacket potato per person.

Roasted lemongrass chicken

Serves 4

213 calories per serving

Takes 20 minutes to prepare
+ marinating overnight,
1¼ hours to cook

**3 fresh lemongrass stalks,
outer layers removed and
chopped**
2 garlic cloves
**5 cm (2 inches) fresh root
ginger, peeled and chopped**
1 shallot
1 tablespoon caster sugar
½ teaspoon dried chilli flakes
2 tablespoons Thai fish sauce
1 tablespoon light soy sauce
juice and grated zest of a lime
1.5 kg (3 lb 5 oz) chicken
**salt and freshly ground black
pepper**

*An exotic lemongrass paste infuses the whole chicken with
flavour as it marinates overnight.*

1 Put the lemongrass, garlic, ginger, shallot, sugar, chilli flakes,
fish sauce, soy sauce, lime juice and zest in a food processor,
or use a hand blender, and whizz to a paste. Season.

2 Gently run your hands under the skin of the chicken to
detach it from the carcass. Make 2–3 slashes in each leg.
Rub the marinade under the skin and all over the top of the
chicken then put it in a plastic bag and seal. Put it on a plate
and leave to marinate in the fridge for at least 8 hours or
overnight.

3 Preheat the oven to Gas Mark 4/180°C/fan oven 160°C.
Put the chicken in a roasting tin and spoon any marinade
left in the bag over the top. Roast the chicken for 1¼ hours,
occasionally basting it with the juices in the tin, until cooked
and there is no trace of pink when the thickest part of the
chicken is pierced with a skewer.

4 Remove the chicken from the oven, cover it with foil and
leave to rest for 10 minutes before carving.

Pot-roast chicken with fennel

Serves 4

273 calories per serving

Takes 20 minutes to prepare,
1¼ hours to cook

calorie controlled cooking
spray

**1.5 kg (3 lb 5 oz) whole
chicken**

**1 fennel bulb, stalks
discarded, halved and cut
into 1 cm (½ inch) slices**

**1 large carrot, peeled and
quartered**

1 large leek, sliced

1 onion, halved

10 fresh thyme sprigs

2 bay leaves

**2 garlic cloves, flattened with
the side of a knife**

1 teaspoon sugar

200 ml (7 fl oz) dry white wine

salt and freshly ground black
pepper

*A neat way to cook a chicken and all the vegetables in one
go, this makes a delicious summer main course.*

1 Preheat the oven to Gas Mark 4/180°C/fan oven 160°C.
Spray a flameproof casserole dish with the cooking spray.
Season the chicken and brown it over a medium heat, turning
occasionally, until it is browned all over – this will take about
10 minutes and is a bit fiddly.

2 Arrange the fennel, carrot, leek, onion, thyme, bay leaves
and garlic around the chicken. Mix the sugar into the wine then
pour over the chicken, season, and bring up to the boil. Cover
the casserole and transfer to the oven.

3 Cook for 45 minutes, then remove the lid and cook for
another 20–30 minutes until the top of the chicken is browned
and cooked.

4 Remove the chicken from the dish and leave to stand for
5 minutes before carving. Serve the chicken without skin, with
the vegetables and garlic.

Tip… Serve with 100 g (3½ oz) boiled potatoes per person.

Finger-licking chicken

Serves 8

145 calories per serving

Takes 5 minutes to prepare
+ 20 minutes marinating,
30 minutes to cook

❄

16 x 75 g (2¾ oz) skinless
chicken drumsticks

6 tablespoons light soy sauce

finely grated zest and juice of
a lime

2 teaspoons chilli flakes

2 teaspoons grated fresh root
ginger

2 teaspoons tomato purée

2 teaspoons artificial
sweetener

*These drumsticks make great finger food for bonfire night
or a barbecue – make sure you serve them with plenty of
paper napkins.*

1 Put the drumsticks in a non-metallic ovenproof dish. Mix
together the remaining ingredients and pour over the meat.
Leave to marinate for 20 minutes.

2 Preheat the oven to Gas Mark 5/190°C/fan oven 170°C.
Bake the chicken in the marinade for 30 minutes until golden
and the juice runs clear when a skewer is inserted. Serve two
chicken drumsticks each with the marinade to dip into.

Variation... Try this with 800 g (1 lb 11 oz) skinless,
boneless chicken breasts in place of the drumsticks. Cut
the chicken into strips and marinate as above. Thread on to
16 skewers (see Tip on page 46) and grill for 5–10 minutes
until golden.

Saffron chicken with apricots

Serves 4

415 calories per serving

Takes 10 minutes to prepare,
25–30 minutes to cook

❄

a pinch of saffron threads

250 ml (9 fl oz) hot chicken
stock

calorie controlled cooking spray

1 large onion, sliced

2 garlic cloves, sliced

2 x 165 g (5¾ oz) skinless,
boneless chicken breasts,
chopped into bite size pieces

1 teaspoon ground cumin

1 teaspoon turmeric

1 teaspoon ground coriander

1 teaspoon paprika

75 g (2¾ oz) dried apricots,
halved

150 g (5½ oz) canned chick
peas, drained and rinsed

175 g (6 oz) couscous

1 tablespoon chopped fresh
mint

1 tablespoon chopped fresh
flat leaf parsley

salt and freshly ground black
pepper

50 g (1¾ oz) toasted flaked
almonds, to serve

*Serve this fruity spicy chicken with couscous for an easy
supper with friends.*

1 Stir the saffron threads into the chicken stock and leave to
one side.

2 Heat a medium pan, spray with cooking spray and sauté the
onion and garlic for 3–4 minutes until starting to soften. Add
the chicken pieces and cook for another 3–4 minutes, stirring
occasionally. Add all the spices and stir to coat the chicken.

3 Pour in the stock and saffron and add the apricots and
chick peas. Bring to a simmer and continue to simmer for
15–20 minutes, until the chicken is cooked through.

4 Meanwhile, place the couscous in a large bowl and add just
enough boiling water to cover. Leave to stand for 10 minutes.
Just before serving, stir with a fork to break up any lumps.

5 Check the chicken and apricot seasoning and stir in the
chopped herbs. Serve on a bed of couscous sprinkled with
the toasted almond flakes.

Spinach and chicken pilaff

Serves 4
333 calories per serving
Takes 22 minutes

2 eggs
calorie controlled cooking
    spray
1 onion, chopped finely
225 g (8 oz) cooked lean
    chicken, shredded
a generous pinch of saffron
    threads
1½ tablespoons mild curry
    powder
200 g (7 oz) basmati rice
125 g (4½ oz) frozen chopped
    spinach
15 g (½ oz) toasted pine nut
    kernels
salt and freshly ground black
    pepper

*This is delicious hot – and any leftovers make an ideal
packed lunch the next day.*

1 Put the eggs in a small saucepan and cover with boiling
water. Bring back to the boil and cook for 7 minutes. Drain and
set aside.

2 Meanwhile, spray a wide, lidded, non-stick saucepan with
cooking spray. Add the onion and cook for 3–4 minutes until
starting to soften. Stir in the chicken, saffron, curry powder
and rice and cook for 1 minute.

3 Stir in 600 ml (20 fl oz) boiling water with the frozen spinach.
Cover and simmer for 10 minutes until the rice is al dente and
the water has been absorbed. Season to taste.

4 Meanwhile, peel the eggs and cut into quarters. Serve the
pilaff in bowls topped with the egg quarters and sprinkled with
the pine nut kernels.

♥ Variation… Replace the chicken with 350 g (12 oz)
Quorn Chicken Style Pieces.

Tip… Serve with a cubed tomato and coriander salad.

Suppers for one and two

Balsamic chicken pizza

Serves 2
366 calories per serving
Takes 30 minutes to prepare,
12 minutes to cook

**23 cm (9 inch) ready-made
thin and crispy pizza base**

For the topping
**calorie controlled cooking
spray**
1 small onion, chopped finely
**400 g can cherry tomatoes in
juice**
**1 tablespoon chopped fresh
basil leaves**
**100 g (3½ oz) skinless,
boneless chicken breast,
chopped into 1 cm (½ inch)
pieces**
**2 tablespoons balsamic
vinegar**
**1 yellow pepper, de-seeded
and sliced (optional)**
**75 g (2¾ oz) light mozzarella,
drained and torn into pieces**
**salt and freshly ground black
pepper**
fresh basil leaves, to garnish

*Share a sophisticated pizza for two made with a ready-
made base.*

1 To make the tomato sauce for the topping, spray a medium
saucepan with the cooking spray and set over a medium heat.
Add the onion and cook for about 5–7 minutes until softened,
adding a little water if necessary. Add the tomatoes and basil.
Bring to the boil and simmer for 20–25 minutes until thickened.
Season and set aside.

2 Preheat the oven to Gas Mark 7/220°C/fan oven 200°C.
Meanwhile, put the chicken pieces in a small bowl with 1
tablespoon of the balsamic vinegar and set aside for 10
minutes to marinate.

3 Spray a small non-stick frying pan with the cooking
spray and place over a high heat. Add the chicken and the
vinegar marinade. Cook, stirring, for about 3–5 minutes until
the chicken is cooked through and most of the vinegar has
evaporated. Add the remaining vinegar. Stir to deglaze the pan.
Allow the vinegar to reduce for 1–2 minutes until it just coats
the chicken, then remove from the heat.

4 Spray a non-stick baking tray with cooking spray and put the
pizza base on it. Spread the pizza base with the tomato sauce.
Scatter with the chicken pieces and pepper, if using. Drizzle
with any reduced vinegar left in the pan and top with the
mozzarella. Bake for 10–12 minutes until the base is golden
and the cheese is bubbling. Serve immediately, garnished with
basil leaves.

Bacon wrapped chicken with steamed vegetables

Serves 1
255 calories per serving
Takes 1 hour
❄

1 lean back bacon rasher
1 chicken breast
½ a shallot, cubed finely
100 ml (3½ fl oz) chicken stock
1 small carrot, sliced thinly
25 g (1 oz) mange tout
50 g (1¾ oz) broccoli florets
25 g (1 oz) swede, chopped
2 teaspoons low fat soft cheese
freshly ground black pepper

Treat yourself to this tasty supper for one.

1 Preheat the oven to Gas Mark 6/200°C/fan oven 180°C. Place the bacon on a chopping board and stretch it with the your hands. Wrap it around the chicken breast. Season with freshly ground black pepper.

2 Fry the chicken breast in a frying pan over a medium heat, with the shallot, for 5–6 minutes on each side. Put the chicken and shallot in a small ovenproof dish and pour over the stock. Cover and cook in the oven for 15–20 minutes.

3 Put all the vegetables in a steamer (see Tip below) and cook for 10–12 minutes until tender.

4 Keep the chicken warm and pour off the stock into a small pan; stir in the soft cheese and bring to a boil for 2–3 minutes to reduce the liquid.

5 Serve the chicken, sliced, on a bed of the vegetables with the sauce poured over the top.

Tip… To steam vegetables, cut them into even, bite size chunks and place them in a metal steamer – or use a colander if you don't have a steamer. Half fill a saucepan with water and bring to the boil. Place the steamer over the boiling water, being careful not to let it touch the water. Cover with a lid and steam the vegetables for 10–15 minutes until tender.

Chicken with mushroom and Marsala sauce

Serves 2

231 calories per serving

Takes 25 minutes to prepare,
20 minutes to cook

❄

**2 x 165 g (5¾ oz) skinless,
boneless chicken breasts**

4 fresh sage leaves

**calorie controlled cooking
spray**

**4 tablespoons Marsala or
medium sherry**

**100 g (3½ oz) mushrooms,
sliced**

**225 ml (8 fl oz) chicken or
vegetable stock**

freshly ground black pepper

*Mushrooms and Marsala combined in a classic sauce for
chicken.*

1 Using a sharp knife, cut a pocket into each chicken breast.
Stuff two sage leaves into each pocket. Close the pockets and
secure with cocktail sticks.

2 Heat a non-stick frying pan and spray with the cooking
spray. Add the chicken breasts and cook on each side for 2–3
minutes, until seared and lightly browned. Pour in the Marsala
or sherry and allow it to bubble up for a few seconds. Add the
mushrooms and stock, then season. Partially cover the pan and
simmer over a low heat for 20 minutes, turning the chicken
after 10 minutes.

3 To test that the chicken is ready, pierce it with a sharp knife
or skewer; the juices should run clear. If there is any trace
of pink, cook for a few more minutes. Serve the chicken and
mushrooms with the sauce poured over.

Variation... Use 2 x 150 g (5½ oz) turkey breast steaks
instead of chicken.

Chicken and broccoli conchiglie

Serves 1
446 calories per serving
Takes 20 minutes

40 g (1½ oz) dried conchiglie or pasta shells

110 g (4 oz) long stemmed broccoli or broccoli florets, trimmed

calorie controlled cooking spray

150 g (5½ oz) skinless, boneless chicken breast, cut into strips

1 small red onion, sliced

½ red pepper, de-seeded and sliced

2 tablespoons light soy sauce

1 tablespoon sweet Thai chilli sauce

salt and freshly ground black pepper

fresh coriander leaves, to garnish

Conchiglie are ridged pasta shells. They're available in different sizes and sometimes they are multicoloured too.

1 Bring a large pan of water to the boil, add the pasta and cook for 10–12 minutes or according to the packet instructions. Add the broccoli for the final 5 minutes of cooking time. Drain and rinse thoroughly.

2 Spray a non-stick frying pan with the cooking spray and heat until hot. Add the chicken, onion and red pepper. Stir fry for 5 minutes until browned and cooked through.

3 Add the soy sauce and chilli sauce. Toss to coat. Stir in the pasta and broccoli and cook for 1 minute until everything is piping hot. Season and serve garnished with coriander leaves.

Tip… Long stemmed or purple sprouting broccoli has especially tender stems. It's available in spring and summer.

Ⓥ Variation… For a veggie version, use 1 x 50 g (1¾ oz) Quorn Fillet, sliced.

Chicken fricassée

Serves 2
385 calories per serving
Takes 35 minutes

100 g (3½ oz) brown rice
calorie controlled cooking
   spray
2 x 125 g (4½ oz) skinless,
   boneless chicken breasts
300 ml (10 fl oz) chicken stock
110 g (4 oz) carrots, cut into
   thick chunks
150 g (5½ oz) button
   mushrooms, sliced
1 garlic clove, crushed
75 g (2¾ oz) low fat soft
   cheese

This recipe uses low fat soft cheese, which reduces the fat content but keeps the creamy taste.

1 Bring a pan of water to the boil and cook the rice according to the packet instructions. Drain well and leave to cool.

2 Meanwhile, lightly coat a deep, lidded, non-stick frying pan with the cooking spray and heat until hot. Add the chicken and cook for 3–4 minutes until browned all over. Add the stock and carrots. Bring to the boil, cover and simmer for 10–15 minutes until tender.

3 Meanwhile, lightly coat another small non-stick frying pan with cooking spray. Add the mushrooms and cook, stirring, for 5 minutes until the juices have been released and evaporated. Add the garlic and cooked rice and cook for a further minute, until hot. Divide between two plates.

4 Remove the chicken and carrots from the frying pan with a slotted spoon, reserving the stock. Place the chicken and carrots on top of the rice and keep the plates warm. Return the pan with the stock to the hob. Boil quickly for 1 minute. Remove from the heat and stir in the soft cheese. Pour the sauce over the chicken.

Chicken cacciatore

Serves 2
345 calories per serving
Takes 25 minutes to prepare,
20 minutes to cook
✳

**calorie controlled cooking
spray**
**285 g (10 oz) skinless,
boneless chicken breasts,
cut into large bite size
pieces**
1 onion, sliced
**40 g (1½ oz) lean back bacon,
cubed**
2 garlic cloves, chopped
100 ml (3½ fl oz) white wine
400 g can chopped tomatoes
1 teaspoon tomato purée
1 bay leaf
**1 tablespoon fresh thyme
leaves, plus extra sprigs to
garnish**
**90 g (3¼ oz) canned cannellini
beans, drained and rinsed**
**1 tablespoon capers in brine,
drained and rinsed**
**salt and freshly ground black
pepper**

Italian-style hunter's chicken is a filling supper dish.

1 Heat a large lidded casserole dish, spray with the cooking
spray, add the chicken and sauté for 3 minutes until browned
all over. Add the onion to the casserole dish. Cook for 3 minutes
until softened, stirring occasionally. Add the bacon and cook
for 3 minutes until golden and crisp. Stir in the garlic and
cook for another minute.

2 Add the wine and boil gently for about 5 minutes until
reduced by three-quarters. Add the chopped tomatoes, tomato
purée, bay leaf, thyme and 3 tablespoons of water. Bring to
the boil then reduce the heat and stir in the beans and capers.
Simmer, partially covered, for 20 minutes, stirring occasionally,
until reduced and cooked through. Season to taste and serve
garnished with thyme.

☻ Variation… For a vegetarian alternative, omit the
chicken and bacon and increase the quantity of cannellini
beans to a 400 g can, drained and rinsed.

Chicken, porcini and sage risotto

Serves 2

428 calories per serving

Takes 35 minutes +
  30 minutes soaking

❄

250 ml (9 fl oz) boiling water

25 g (1 oz) dried porcini
  mushrooms

calorie controlled cooking
  spray

125 g (4½ oz) risotto rice

4 tablespoons dry white wine

200 g (7 oz) skinless, boneless
  chicken breasts, chopped
  into 2 cm (¾ inch) pieces

1 garlic clove, crushed

1 small leek, sliced thinly

2–3 fresh sage leaves

600 ml (20 fl oz) hot vegetable
  stock

25 g (1 oz) frozen peas,
  defrosted

2 teaspoons finely grated
  Parmesan cheese

freshly ground black pepper

Serve this creamy risotto for a date-night supper.

1 Pour the boiling water over the porcini mushrooms and leave to soak for at least 30 minutes.

2 Spray a large non-stick frying pan or saucepan with the cooking spray. Add the rice and cook over a low heat for 1–2 minutes, stirring all the time, until the rice looks glossy, but not brown. Add the white wine to the pan and let it bubble for a few moments, then add the chicken, garlic, leek and sage leaves. Pour in the soaked mushrooms along with their liquid, then add a ladleful of stock. Stir well.

3 Cook over a medium heat for 20–25 minutes, stirring often, and gradually add the remaining stock, until the rice has absorbed all the liquid and has a nice creamy texture. If necessary, add a little extra stock or water.

4 Add the peas, stirring gently to mix them in. Check the seasoning, then share the risotto between two warm plates or bowls. Sprinkle each portion with 1 teaspoon of Parmesan cheese and serve.

Ⓥ Variation… Omit the chicken to make a vegetarian risotto.

Chicken rice salad

Serves 1

311 calories per serving

Takes 10 minutes to prepare,
20–25 minutes to cook

300 ml (½ pint) chicken or
vegetable stock

50 g (1¾ oz) brown rice

75 g (2¾ oz) cooked, skinless
boneless chicken breast,
sliced

8 red seedless grapes, halved

1 spring onion, sliced

1 teaspoon orange zest

2 teaspoons white balsamic
(or ordinary balsamic)
vinegar

Brown rice is more filling than white. Cook it in stock to add extra flavour. White balsamic vinegar makes the salad look nicer as it doesn't colour the food.

1 In a lidded saucepan, bring the stock to the boil and add the rice. Cover and cook for 20–25 minutes until tender. Drain any excess stock and leave to cool, then chill the rice in the fridge.

2 When ready to serve, stir in the chicken, grapes and spring onion. Mix together the orange zest and balsamic vinegar, then stir into the rice salad.

Tips... You can make this salad the night before, then leave it in the fridge to let the flavours mingle. Spice it up with 1 teaspoon of freshly chopped red chilli.

Lemon and ginger chicken

Serves 2
283 calories per serving
Takes 30 minutes

4 teaspoons light soy sauce
2 teaspoons clear honey
grated zest and juice of ½ a small lemon
1 teaspoon cornflour
20 g (¾ oz) cashew nuts
250 g (9 oz) skinless, boneless chicken breast, cut into strips
calorie controlled cooking spray
½ onion, sliced
1 teaspoon finely grated fresh root ginger
50 g (1¾ oz) baby corn, halved lengthways
60 g (2 oz) sugar snap peas

Lemon juice, ginger and honey add zing to this chicken and vegetable stir-fry.

1 Mix together the soy sauce, honey, lemon zest and juice, and cornflour in a shallow dish.

2 Put the cashews in a wok or non-stick frying pan and dry fry, turning occasionally, for 3–4 minutes until light golden. Set aside.

3 Reheat the wok or non-stick frying pan until hot, spray the chicken with the cooking spray and stir-fry for 5–6 minutes until golden all over. Remove from the pan and transfer the chicken to the soy sauce mixture and turn until coated.

4 Spray the pan with the cooking spray and stir-fry the onion for 3 minutes. Add the ginger, baby corn and sugar snap peas then cook for a further 2 minutes. Return the chicken to the pan with the soy mixture and stir-fry for 1–2 minutes until the sauce is reduced and thickened. Serve topped with the toasted cashews.

Ⓥ Variation… Replace the chicken with 175 g (6 oz) Quorn Pieces. Marinate in the soy mixture for 15 minutes then add to the stir-fry in step 4 with the onion.

Chilli chicken with Thai-style salad

Serves 2

214 calories per serving

Takes 30 minutes + 30 minutes marinating

2 x 165 g (5¾ oz) skinless, boneless chicken breasts

2 tablespoons sweet chilli sauce

2 tablespoons light soy sauce

2.5 cm (1 inch) fresh root ginger, peeled and grated

calorie controlled cooking spray

50 g (1¾ oz) red cabbage, shredded

50 g (1¾ oz) white cabbage, shredded

1 carrot, grated

1 spring onion, chopped finely

2 tablespoons Thai fish sauce

juice of ½ a lime

1 teaspoon caster sugar

salt and freshly ground black pepper

Fill up on chicken cooked in a sweet chilli marinade and a big crunchy salad.

1 Put the chicken between two sheets of cling film and, using the end of a rolling pin or meat mallet, flatten it until it's about 2 cm (¾ inch) thick.

2 Mix together the sweet chilli sauce and soy sauce in a large, shallow dish. Using your hands, squeeze the juice from the ginger into the bowl, season and then add the chicken. Turn it to coat it in the marinade then cover and leave in the fridge for at least 30 minutes.

3 Meanwhile, put the red and white cabbage, carrot and spring onion in a serving bowl. Mix together the fish sauce, lime juice and sugar, until the latter has dissolved, and then pour it over the vegetables. Season and toss until coated in the dressing.

4 Heat a non-stick frying pan until hot. Spray the chicken with the cooking spray and cook over a medium heat for 8–10 minutes, turning once, until cooked through. Serve the chicken with the cabbage.

Tip… This dish works particularly well with fish, too. Swap the chicken for 2 x 175 g (6 oz) thick fillets of pollock and marinate and cook it in the same way.

Marinated chicken with sweet potatoes

Serves 2

415 calories per serving

Takes 20 minutes to prepare
+ 1 hour marinating,
35 minutes to cook

**2 small red onions, cut into
wedges**

**grated zest and juice of ½ a
lemon**

**2 tablespoons low fat natural
yogurt**

½ teaspoon smoked paprika

1 teaspoon fresh thyme leaves

**450 g (1 lb) skinless chicken
drumsticks**

**calorie controlled cooking
spray**

**300 g (10½ oz) sweet
potatoes, unpeeled and cut
into wedges**

**1 large red pepper, de-seeded
and cut into large chunks**

6 whole garlic cloves

**a generous handful of rocket
leaves**

**salt and freshly ground black
pepper**

lemon wedges, to serve

*The spicy yogurt marinade in this recipe not only flavours
the meat, it also prevents it from drying out.*

1 Put a couple of the onion wedges in a food processor, with
the lemon zest and juice, yogurt, paprika, thyme and seasoning
and whizz until smooth. Pour over the chicken, cover and
leave to marinate for 1 hour at room temperature, or in the
fridge for longer.

2 Preheat the oven to Gas Mark 6/200°C/fan oven 180°C. Spray
a medium non-stick roasting tin with the cooking spray and
add the sweet potatoes, red pepper, remaining onion wedges
and garlic. Add the marinated drumsticks and spray lightly with
the cooking spray again to encourage the vegetables to brown.

3 Roast for 30–35 minutes until the chicken and vegetables
are cooked through. Serve topped with the rocket leaves and
lemon wedges for squeezing over.

Tip… To remove the skin from a chicken drumstick, hold
the skin at the thick end of the drumstick and pull it down
so the skin is virtually inside out, but still attached at the
thin bony end. Snip the skin off with scissors to remove it
completely.

Paprika chicken

Serves 2

256 calories per serving

Takes 15 minutes to prepare, 10 minutes to cook

2 teaspoons chicken gravy granules

1 tablespoon paprika

4 x 80 g (3 oz) skinless, boneless chicken thighs

calorie controlled cooking spray

2 tablespoons Worcestershire sauce

1 tablespoon tomato purée

Chicken thighs are full of flavour and really moist, especially cooked this way.

1 Crush the gravy granules and paprika in a pestle and mortar to a fine powder. Put the chicken thighs on a plate and sprinkle with the paprika powder, turning to coat thoroughly.

2 Heat a wide, lidded saucepan until hot. Spray the chicken thighs with the cooking spray and cook them for 5 minutes until browned. Add the Worcestershire sauce, tomato purée and 200 ml (7 fl oz) cold water. Bring to the boil, cover and simmer for 10 minutes, turning halfway through, until cooked.

3 Remove the chicken thighs with a pair of tongs. Put them on a plate and cover with foil. Rapidly bubble the sauce for 1–2 minutes until thickened. Pour over the chicken and serve immediately.

Tips... Serve with 150 g (5½ oz) cooked new potatoes per person and cooked sugar snap peas. If you prefer, you can use 2 x 165 g (5¾ oz) skinless, boneless chicken breasts instead.

Quick herby chicken curry

Serves 2
219 calories per serving
Takes 15 minutes

calorie controlled cooking
  spray
1 small onion, sliced
2 x 125 g (4½ oz) skinless,
  boneless chicken breasts,
  cubed
2 garlic cloves, crushed
1 teaspoon grated fresh root
  ginger
1 teaspoon garam masala or
  medium curry powder
2 teaspoons cornflour
150 g (5½ oz) low fat natural
  yogurt
1 tablespoon chopped fresh
  mint
3 heaped tablespoons
  chopped fresh coriander

Fresh herbs are the key to this fragrant curry.

1 Heat a non-stick frying pan until hot and spray with the cooking spray. Fry the onion for about 4 minutes, then push to one side and add the chicken to the pan. Cook for 3–4 minutes, stirring the chicken and onion around once or twice.

2 Add the garlic, ginger and garam masala or curry powder and cook for 1 minute, stirring. Remove the pan from the hob.

3 Blend the cornflour with 1 teaspoon of cold water and then stir this into the yogurt and gradually stir the yogurt mixture into the pan, one spoonful at a time. Return the pan to the hob and gently bring to a simmer, taking care not to boil the sauce or it may curdle. Stir in the herbs just before serving.

ⓥ **Variation…** Try 250 g (9 oz) Quorn Deli Chicken Style Pieces instead of chicken.

Tip… Try growing your own herbs, such as thyme, basil, parsley, chives and coriander, on a sunny windowsill – they'll always be handy and it's far more economical than buying packets of cut herbs from the supermarket that have a short shelf-life.

Salsa chicken with beans and rice

Serves 2
595 calories per serving
Takes 15 minutes to prepare,
18 minutes to cook

300 g jar salsa
200 ml (7 fl oz) chicken stock
300 g (10½ oz) butternut squash, de-seeded and cut into chunks
1 red pepper, de-seeded and cut into chunks
75 g (2¾ oz) basmati rice
15 g (½ oz) chopped fresh coriander
300 g (10½ oz) skinless, boneless chicken breast, cut into chunks
410 g can red kidney beans in water, drained and rinsed

This couldn't be simpler to make. A jar of Mexican salsa forms the base – choose a mild or a hot one, depending on your taste.

1 Tip half of the jar of salsa into a lidded pan and pour in the stock. Add the squash and pepper; cover and simmer for 10 minutes.

2 Add the rice, half the coriander and the chicken, then cover the pan and cook gently for about 8 minutes until the rice is tender and the chicken is cooked through.

3 Stir in the beans. Cover and leave for a few minutes to warm through. Serve with the remaining salsa and scatter with the rest of the coriander.

Spicy chicken skewers

Serves 1

375 calories per serving

Takes 35 minutes + marinating

1 tablespoon low fat natural yogurt

2 tablespoons soy sauce

1 garlic clove, crushed

1 teaspoon tomato purée

a few drops of Tabasco sauce

150 g (5½ oz) skinless, boneless chicken breast, cut into chunks

4 cherry tomatoes

1 red pepper, de-seeded and cut into chunks

½ a red onion, sliced into wedges

4 mushrooms

For the pea 'guacamole'

100 g (3½ oz) fresh peas or frozen peas, defrosted

juice of ½ a lime

½ a small red onion, cubed finely

2 tablespoons low fat plain yogurt

salt and freshly ground black pepper

Combine with your favourite summer vegetables for a colourful and flavourful meal.

1 In a small bowl mix together the yogurt, soy sauce, garlic, tomato purée and Tabasco sauce. Add the chicken and stir to coat. Cover the bowl and leave to marinate for at least 10 minutes, but up to 2 hours, in the fridge.

2 Preheat the grill to hot or light the barbecue. Thread the chicken and vegetables on to skewers (see Tip on page 46) and cook under the grill or over a barbecue for 10–15 minutes, turning regularly, until the vegetables start to char on the edges and the chicken is cooked right through.

3 Meanwhile make the pea guacamole by blending all the ingredients in a food processor until smooth. Serve with the chicken and vegetable skewers.

Weekday chicken and 'chips'

Serves 2

340 calories per serving

Takes 20 minutes to prepare,
  30 minutes to cook

**calorie controlled cooking
  spray**

**200 g (7 oz) new potatoes,
  scrubbed and sliced into
  5 mm (¼ inch) rounds**

**1 small onion, cut into
  8 wedges**

**2 x 150 g (5½ oz) skinless,
  boneless chicken breasts**

6 small bay leaves

**1 small red pepper, de-seeded
  and sliced into long strips**

6 baby plum tomatoes

2 garlic cloves, unpeeled

a few fresh thyme sprigs

**2 tablespoons extra light
  mayonnaise**

½ teaspoon harissa paste

1 teaspoon lemon juice

**salt and freshly ground black
  pepper**

*Roasted until crisp, the new potato chips and succulent
chicken breasts are served with a spicy garlic mayonnaise.*

1 Preheat the oven to Gas Mark 6/200°C/fan oven 180°C.
Spray a 23 x 35 cm (9 x 14 inch) baking dish with the cooking
spray. Arrange the potatoes and onion in a single layer in the
dish, then spray again with the cooking spray. Place in the oven
for 5 minutes while you brown the chicken.

2 Heat a non-stick frying pan, spray the chicken with the
cooking spray and cook over a medium heat for about 5 minutes,
turning once, until golden. Remove the chicken from the pan
and make three slashes diagonally across the top of each
breast. Place a bay leaf in each cut.

3 Remove the dish from the oven, turn the potatoes, and
arrange the pepper, plum tomatoes and garlic in the dish,
scatter with sprigs of thyme, then top with the chicken
breasts and season. Return the dish to the oven and roast for
20 minutes, then remove the garlic cloves and set aside. Roast
the chicken for further 5–10 minutes or until cooked through
and the potatoes turn golden and slightly crisp.

4 Squeeze the garlic out of its skin into a bowl, then mash with
a fork. Stir in the mayonnaise, harissa paste and lemon juice.
Remove the thyme and bay leaves and serve the chicken,
potatoes and vegetables with a spoonful of roasted garlic mayo.

ⓥ Variation... Use 200 g (7 oz) Quorn Fillets instead.
No need to brown them, simply place on the potatoes in
step 3, spray with the cooking spray and top with bay
leaves. Cook for 20–25 minutes until golden.

From around the world

Chicken chow mein

Serves 4

474 calories per serving

Takes 25 minutes to prepare +
30 minutes marinating,
10 minutes to cook

**600 g (1 lb 5 oz) skinless,
boneless chicken breasts,
cut into strips**

6 tablespoons soy sauce

200 g (7 oz) dried egg noodles

**calorie controlled cooking
spray**

1 large onion, sliced

**1 carrot, halved crossways
and cut into batons**

**100 g (3½ oz) baby corn,
halved lengthways**

100 g (3½ oz) sugar snap peas

**2 large garlic cloves, sliced
thinly**

**2.5 cm (1 inch) fresh root
ginger, peeled and chopped
finely**

**150 g (5½ oz) Chinese leaves,
sliced thinly**

**2 tablespoons Chinese
cooking wine or dry sherry**

4 tablespoons oyster sauce

freshly ground black pepper

*Chow mein simply means 'stir-fried noodles'. This popular
dish is tasty and very quick to make.*

1 Marinate the chicken in 4 tablespoons of soy sauce for
30 minutes. Bring a pan of water to the boil and cook the
noodles according to the packet instructions, then drain and
refresh under cold running water. Place in a bowl, cover with
cold water, and set aside.

2 Remove the chicken from the soy sauce and discard the
marinade. Heat a large wok or non-stick frying pan, add
the chicken, spray with the cooking spray and stir-fry for
4–5 minutes until golden and cooked. Remove from the pan
and set aside.

3 Add the onion, carrot, baby corn and sugar snap peas to the
pan, spray with the cooking spray and stir-fry for 3 minutes.
Add the garlic, ginger and Chinese leaves and stir-fry for
another minute.

4 Drain the cooked noodles and add to the pan with the
Chinese cooking wine or sherry, the remaining soy sauce,
oyster sauce and chicken and stir until combined and heated
through. Season with black pepper, then serve in large
shallow bowls.

⊙ **Variation...** Replace the chicken with 150 g (5½ oz)
chestnut mushrooms, quartered, and 150 g (5½ oz)
tenderstem broccoli and add them in step 3 with the
other vegetables.

Chicken enchiladas

Serves 4

523 calories per serving

Takes 30 minutes to prepare, 25 minutes to cook

300 g (10½ oz) skinless chicken breasts

300 ml (½ pint) hot chicken stock

calorie controlled cooking spray

1 onion, chopped

1 green pepper, de-seeded and cubed

30 g sachet taco seasoning mix

250 g (9 oz) low fat natural cottage cheese, sieved

75 g (2¾ oz) half fat mature Cheddar cheese, grated finely

500 ml (18 fl oz) passata

¼ teaspoon hot chilli powder

2 garlic cloves, crushed

8 x 20 cm (8 inch) flour tortillas

Enchiladas are a classic Tex Mex food, made by wrapping a tortilla around a meat and cheese filling, then baked with a spicy tomato sauce and extra cheese.

1 Simmer the chicken breasts in the hot stock for 15 minutes, until completely cooked through. Reserving the liquid, remove the chicken and allow to cool, then tear the meat into thin shreds. Preheat the oven to Gas Mark 4/180°C/fan oven 160°C.

2 Spray a non-stick pan with the cooking spray and heat the pan. Add the onion and pepper and cook for 5 minutes until softened. Stir in the shredded chicken, taco seasoning and chicken poaching liquid. Cover and simmer for 10 minutes.

3 Mix the sieved cottage cheese with half of the grated cheese and set aside. Heat the passata, chilli powder and garlic together in a pan and simmer for 10 minutes.

4 Warm the tortillas for 15 seconds on full power in the microwave or for 20 seconds each side in a dry frying pan.

5 Place one eighth of the chicken filling down the centre of each tortilla and spoon one eighth of the cottage cheese mixture on top. Roll up and place in an ovenproof dish, seam side down.

6 Pour the chilli tomato sauce over the filled tortillas and scatter the remaining cheese on top. Bake for 25 minutes. Serve two enchiladas per person.

🌱 **Variation…** Use 250 g (9 oz) Quorn Mince in place of the cooked chicken and vegetable stock instead of chicken.

Cajun chicken goujons

Serves 4

365 calories per serving

Takes 35 minutes + 20
  minutes marinating

❄

450 g (1 lb) skinless,
  boneless chicken breasts,
  cut into strips

2 tablespoons Cajun spice mix

100 ml (3½ fl oz) low fat
  natural yogurt

finely grated zest of 2 limes

2 tablespoons chopped fresh
  coriander

225 g (8 oz) easy-cook rice

75 g (2¾ oz) canned
  sweetcorn, drained

salt

Head to the southern states for these spicy chicken strips.

1 Place the chicken in a shallow dish. Mix together the Cajun spice mix, yogurt, zest of 1 lime and the coriander. Spoon this over the chicken. Stir well to coat all the strips. Cover and leave to marinate for 20 minutes.

2 Meanwhile, cook the rice in lightly salted, boiling water for 12 minutes until tender. Drain and mix the rice with the remaining lime zest and the sweetcorn. Cover and keep warm. Preheat the grill to hot.

3 Grill the chicken for 12–15 minutes, turning frequently, until the chicken is cooked through and slightly browned. Spoon the rice on to four individual serving plates and pile the Cajun chicken on top.

Easy chicken tikka

Serves 4

215 calories per serving

Takes 20 minutes to prepare +
3½ – 4½ hours marinating,
15 minutes to cook

**450 g (1 lb) skinless, boneless
chicken breast, cubed**
150 ml (5 fl oz) wine vinegar
2 garlic cloves, crushed
2 teaspoons chilli powder
**1 teaspoon finely grated fresh
root ginger**
1 teaspoon chopped fresh mint
1 teaspoon garam masala
½ teaspoon cumin seeds
1 tablespoon vegetable oil
**150 g (5½ oz) low fat natural
yogurt**

For the salad and relish
1 red onion, thinly sliced
1 small garlic clove, crushed
**3 tomatoes, skinned,
de-seeded and chopped**
2 tablespoons lemon juice
2 tablespoons chopped mint
**150 g (5 ½ oz) low fat natural
yogurt**
**2 tablespoons chopped fresh
coriander**

*This easy, authentic chicken tikka recipe is perfect for
preparing ahead.*

1 Put the chicken into a non-metallic bowl and add the vinegar
and 1 teaspoon salt. Stir well, then cover and chill in the fridge
for 20–30 minutes.

2 Mix together all the remaining ingredients. Drain the chicken,
discarding the vinegar. Add the yogurt mixture, stirring well,
then cover and chill for at least 3 or 4 hours, or overnight
if preferred.

3 Preheat the grill to hot. To cook, thread the chicken on to
4 skewers (see Tip on page 46) and grill for 12–15 minutes,
turning frequently.

4 To make the tomato and red onion salad, mix the onion with
the garlic, tomatoes, lemon juice and mint. Season with salt
and pepper, transfer to a small bowl and chill thoroughly.

5 To make the coriander relish, mix together the yogurt,
coriander and seasoning. Transfer to a small bowl, cover
and chill. Serve with the chicken tikka and salad.

Tip... This is the perfect recipe for a barbecue. Prepare
the chicken the day before, so that it can absorb the
flavours of the marinade overnight.

Hoisin chicken noodles

Serves 2

428 calories per serving

Takes 10 minutes to prepare,
  10 minutes to cook

**100 g (3½ oz) dried egg
  noodles**

**calorie controlled cooking
  spray**

**2 x 150 g (5½ oz) skinless,
  boneless chicken breasts,
  sliced into thin strips**

**2.5 cm (1 inch) fresh root
  ginger, peeled and cubed
  finely**

2 garlic cloves, cubed finely

**a bunch of spring onions,
  sliced**

**1 red pepper, de-seeded and
  sliced into thin strips**

**2 large handfuls of spinach,
  tough stems removed,
  shredded and washed**

150 ml (5 fl oz) vegetable stock

1 tablespoon soy sauce

2 tablespoons hoisin sauce

To serve

**a small bunch of fresh
  coriander, optional**

**a pinch of dried chilli flakes,
  optional**

*Get dinner on the table in 20 minutes with this super-quick
dish.*

1 Cook the noodles following the packet instructions, then
drain and set aside.

2 Spray a large non-stick frying pan or wok with the cooking
spray and, on a high heat, stir-fry the chicken pieces for a few
minutes, or until white all over and starting to brown.

3 Add the ginger, garlic and spring onions. Stir-fry for a few
more minutes. Add the pepper, spinach, stock and soy sauce.
Stir-fry until the vegetables are slightly softened, browned at
the edges and most of the stock has boiled away.

4 Add the hoisin sauce and stir through with a little more
water, if necessary.

5 Snip the noodles with scissors to make shorter lengths, add
them to the stir-fry and toss together. Serve sprinkled with
fresh coriander and chilli flakes, if using.

Italian chicken casserole

Serves 4
275 calories per serving
Takes 5 minutes to prepare,
  1 hour to cook
❄

1 onion, grated
400 g can chopped tomatoes
200 ml (7 fl oz) chicken stock
1 garlic clove, crushed
1 tablespoon dried mixed
  herbs
4 x 165 g (5¾ oz) chicken
  thighs or drumsticks, skin
  removed
salt and pepper
20 stoned olives, halved, to
  serve

Put this in the oven and sit back and relax while it works its magic. Serve with griddled courgettes.

1 Preheat the oven to Gas Mark 4/180°C/fan oven 160°C. Place all the ingredients except the olives in a casserole dish. Mix well and season to taste. Cover and cook for 1 hour.

2 Stir in the olives just before serving.

Jerk chicken with Caribbean beans

Serves 4
417 calories per serving
Takes 35 minutes

8 x 60 g (2 oz) skinless, boneless chicken fillets
2 tablespoons jerk spice mix
350 g (12 oz) butternut squash, peeled, de-seeded, and cut into 1 cm (½ inch) cubes
calorie controlled cooking spray
1 onion, chopped finely
2 large garlic cloves, chopped finely
1 yellow pepper, de-seeded and cubed
1 teaspoon dried thyme
1 teaspoon cumin seeds
400 g can black beans, drained and rinsed
3 tablespoons chopped fresh coriander
25 g (1 oz) sweet and hot jalapeños from a jar, drained and chopped roughly
salt and freshly ground black pepper

To serve
4 tortillas
4 tablespoons 0% fat Greek yogurt

There's nothing like the taste of the Caribbean to put you in a good mood.

1 Put the chicken fillets on a plate. Sprinkle over the jerk spices, coating both sides, then cover and chill.

2 Bring a pan of water to the boil, add the butternut squash and cook for about 10 minutes or until tender. Drain then refresh under cold running water. Set aside.

3 Meanwhile, heat a lidded non-stick saucepan, spray with the cooking spray and cook the onion for 8 minutes, covered, stirring regularly. Add the garlic, pepper, thyme and cumin seeds. Spray with cooking spray and fry for another 3 minutes, stirring.

4 Preheat the oven to Gas Mark ¼/110°C/fan oven 90°C. Add the black beans, squash and 2 tablespoons of water to the saucepan with the onions and peppers. Stir and heat through for 5 minutes.

5 While the black bean mixture is cooking, heat a griddle or non-stick frying pan, spray the chicken with the cooking spray and cook four of the chicken fillets for 6 minutes, turning once, or until cooked through.

6 When the black beans and squash have finished cooking, season and stir in the coriander and jalapeños.

7 Cover the first batch of cooked chicken and keep warm while you cook the second batch. Meanwhile, wrap the tortillas in foil and warm in the oven. Place a tortilla on each serving plate, top with the black bean mixture then the chicken and a dollop of yogurt.

Lemon chicken Marrakesh

Serves 4

469 calories per serving

Takes 10 minutes to prepare,
50 minutes to cook

❄ (without the couscous)

1 lemon

2 red onions, chopped

1 large fennel bulb, chopped

1 large red pepper, de-seeded
and cubed

600 g (1 lb 5 oz) skinless,
boneless chicken thighs,
trimmed of all visible fat

50 g (1¾ oz) pimento-stuffed
olives in brine, drained
(about 20 olives)

2 large red chillies, sliced

2 garlic cloves, sliced

1 teaspoon ground paprika

2 teaspoons ground cumin

1 tablespoon ground coriander

1 litre (1¾ pints) chicken
stock

200 g (7 oz) couscous

4 tablespoons chopped fresh
flat leaf parsley or coriander
(optional)

salt and freshly ground black
pepper

*Add the couscous to the casserole at the last minute to
soak up the delicious juices – or cook it separately if
you're not eating immediately.*

1 Remove the peel from the lemon with a vegetable peeler
and slice it into matchstick shreds. Put it in a lidded flameproof
casserole dish with the onions, fennel, pepper, chicken, olives,
chillies, garlic, spices and seasoning. Pour the stock into the
pan then cover and simmer for 45 minutes until the chicken is
really tender.

2 Squeeze the juice from the lemon. Tip the couscous, lemon
juice and parsley or coriander, if using, into the casserole. Turn
off the heat and leave for 5 minutes to plump up the couscous
before serving.

Tip... If you enjoy trying new ingredients, you may like to
try Moroccan preserved lemons which are sold in most
supermarkets. Rinse off the salt, chop finely and use to
replace the fresh lemon zest and juice in this recipe.

Mediterranean chicken stew

Serves 6

273 calories per serving

Takes 25 minutes to prepare, 35 minutes to cook

calorie controlled cooking spray

1 onion, sliced finely

3 celery sticks, sliced

500 g (1 lb 2 oz) skinless, boneless chicken thighs, cubed

3 garlic cloves, sliced

1 yellow pepper, de-seeded and sliced

150 ml (5 fl oz) white wine

½ an orange

400 g can chopped tomatoes

a small pinch of saffron threads

600 ml (20 fl oz) hot chicken stock

750 g (1 lb 10 oz) small new potatoes, halved

2 tablespoons cornflour

freshly ground black pepper

This succulent chicken and vegetable stew is bursting with flavour.

1 Heat a lidded, flameproof casserole dish on the hob and spray with the cooking spray. Add the onion and celery and cook for 5 minutes until softened.

2 Meanwhile, heat a non-stick frying pan until hot and spray with the cooking spray. Brown the chicken for about 5 minutes.

3 Add the garlic and pepper to the casserole and cook for 1 minute, stirring. Pour in the wine. Pare a few strips of zest from the orange using a vegetable peeler and add to the casserole. Squeeze the orange juice and add it to the casserole. Boil rapidly for 2 minutes then add the tomatoes, saffron, stock, potatoes and browned chicken. Season with black pepper and bring to the boil. Cover and simmer for 35 minutes.

4 Blend the cornflour with a little cold water and stir into the casserole until the sauce has thickened. Serve in deep plates to hold the sauce.

Tip… Serve the stew with steamed broccoli florets.

Minted chicken with Moroccan couscous

Serves 4

470 calories per serving

Takes 30 minutes + 30
   minutes marinating

❄

A simple yet stunning dish that will go down well at any dinner party.

1 Make vertical slits along the top of each chicken breast. Put them in a shallow non-metallic dish. Mix together the garlic, mint, lemon zest and juice, cinnamon, caster sugar and oil. Drizzle this mixture over the chicken. Cover and leave to marinate for at least 30 minutes.

**4 x 125 g (4½ oz) skinless
   chicken breasts**

2 garlic cloves, chopped

**2 tablespoons chopped fresh
   mint**

**finely grated zest and juice of
   a lemon**

¼ teaspoon ground cinnamon

1 teaspoon caster sugar

2 teaspoons olive oil

275 g (9½ oz) couscous

**350 ml (12 fl oz) boiling
   vegetable stock**

**100 g (3½ oz) ready-to-eat
   dried apricots, chopped
   finely**

**2 tablespoons chopped fresh
   flat leaf parsley**

**150 g (5½ oz) courgettes,
   grated coarsely**

**salt and freshly ground black
   pepper**

2 Meanwhile, put the couscous in a bowl and pour over the hot stock. Fluff up the grains with a fork and cover with cling film. Leave to stand for 15–20 minutes until the grains have absorbed the liquid and are plump. Mix in the chopped apricots, parsley, grated courgettes and seasoning.

3 Preheat the grill. Grill the chicken breasts for 6–8 minutes each side until cooked through. To serve, spoon a mound of couscous on to each plate and top with a chicken breast.

Tips… The longer you leave the chicken to marinate the better the flavour, so if you have time, chill it overnight. Add de-seeded, cubed red and green peppers to the couscous for added colour.

One-pot Moroccan chicken

Serves 2

613 calories per serving

Takes 30 minutes to prepare,
25 minutes to cook

**325 g (11½ oz) skinless,
boneless chicken thighs**

**calorie controlled cooking
spray**

1 large onion, chopped

**½ pointed red pepper,
de-seeded and sliced into
thin rings**

2 garlic cloves, chopped

1 teaspoon ras-el-hanout

1 teaspoon ground coriander

1 teaspoon dried thyme

**100 g (3½ oz) brown basmati
rice**

**150 ml (5 fl oz) unsweetened
orange juice**

**100 ml (3½ fl oz) vegetable
stock**

**salt and freshly ground black
pepper**

To serve

**50 g (1¾ oz) fresh mango,
sliced thinly**

**3 fresh coriander sprigs,
leaves removed**

Cook spicy chicken and rice for two all in one pot.

1 Spray the chicken with the cooking spray. Heat a lidded flameproof casserole dish or heavy based saucepan over a medium heat then brown the chicken for 3 minutes on each side until golden. Remove from the pan and set aside, covered.

2 Spray the casserole dish with the cooking spray. Add the onion then cover and cook for 6 minutes, stirring occasionally, and adding a splash of water if the onion starts to stick. When the onion has softened, stir in the red pepper, garlic, ras-el-hanout, ground coriander, thyme and rice. Cook for 2 minutes until the rice is opaque.

3 Pour in the orange juice and stock, stir and then bring to the boil. Place the chicken on top of the rice and reduce the heat to the lowest setting. Cover and cook for 20–25 minutes or until the rice is tender and the chicken is cooked through.

4 Divide the rice and chicken between two serving plates. Season to taste and scatter the mango and fresh coriander over the top.

Thai-style chicken curry

Serves 4

265 calories per serving

Takes 20 minutes to prepare,
  20 minutes to cook

2 tablespoons finely chopped
  lemongrass, fresh or dried

4 fresh kaffir lime leaves,
  shredded

1 medium leek, sliced thinly

2 teaspoons green Thai curry
  paste

4 x 165 g (5¾ oz) skinless,
  boneless chicken breasts,
  sliced thinly

400 ml (14 fl oz) soya milk

400 ml (14 fl oz) vegetable or
  chicken stock

2 tablespoons soy sauce

1 medium courgette, sliced
  thinly

300 g (10½ oz) green beans,
  halved

400 g (14 oz) pak choi,
  chopped

1 tablespoon lime juice

To garnish

a small bunch of fresh
  coriander, chopped

a small bunch of fresh basil,
  chopped

Full of the flavours of south-east Asia, this quick and easy curry has far fewer calories than a take-away.

1 Mix the lemongrass, lime leaves, leek and curry paste, then heat a medium saucepan and stir-fry the mixture for 2–3 minutes. Add the chicken and stir-fry for another 2 minutes.

2 Add the soya milk, stock and soy sauce and simmer uncovered for 10 minutes. Add the remaining vegetables and cook for another 10 minutes.

3 Add the lime juice and serve the curry in bowls garnished with coriander and basil.

Tip… Kaffir lime leaves can be bought fresh from the fresh herb section of many supermarkets or dried in bottles in the spice section. If using dried leaves, leave them whole and remove them before eating. If you find the fresh leaves, freeze what you don't use in a plastic bag for future use.

Piri piri chicken

Serves 4

231 calories per serving

Takes 15 minutes to prepare
+ 1 hour marinating,
20 minutes to cook

1 large red pepper, de-seeded
and sliced

1 large garlic clove, halved

1 teaspoon paprika

2 tablespoons red wine
vinegar

4 x 165 g (5¾ oz) skinless,
boneless chicken breasts

calorie controlled cooking
spray

salt and freshly ground black
pepper

Portuguese-style chicken with paprika and red pepper.

1 Put the pepper, garlic, paprika, vinegar and seasoning in
a food processor, or use a hand blender, and whizz to make
a coarse paste.

2 Make three slashes diagonally across each chicken breast.
Place in a non metallic roasting dish, spoon over the marinade,
cover and marinate in the fridge for at least 1 hour or overnight,
if time allows.

3 Preheat the oven to Gas Mark 6/200°C/fan oven 180°C. Heat
a large non-stick frying pan, spray the chicken with the cooking
spray, and cook for 2 minutes on each side until browned.

4 Put the chicken in the roasting dish, spoon over more of the
marinade and roast for 15–20 minutes or until cooked through.

Variation… Instead of chicken, marinate 2 x 55 g (1¾ oz)
Quorn Fillets per person for 1 hour. Spray with cooking spray
and pan-fry for about 10 minutes.

Tip… Serve with 40 g (1½ oz) dried wholewheat couscous
per person, cooked according to the packet instructions,
and some salad leaves, dressed in lemon juice.

Quick chicken korma

Serves 4

291 calories per serving

Takes 20 minutes to prepare,
25 minutes to cook

4 cm (1½ inches) fresh root
ginger, peeled and chopped

3 large garlic cloves, chopped

4 cardamom pods, lightly
crushed with the flat blade
of a knife

calorie controlled cooking
spray

1 large onion, chopped finely

60 g (2 oz) chicken korma
paste

1 teaspoon turmeric

200 g (7 oz) canned chopped
tomatoes

200 ml (7 fl oz) vegetable
stock

550 g (1 lb 3 oz) skinless,
boneless chicken breasts,
cut into bite size pieces

12 cherry tomatoes, halved

4 tablespoons Weight Watchers
reduced fat thick cream

salt and freshly ground black
pepper

4 lime wedges, to serve

*With its mild and creamy sauce, korma is one of the most
popular Indian curries.*

1 Place the ginger and garlic in a food processor with
3 tablespoons of water, or use a hand held blender, and whizz
to a paste. Set aside.

2 Heat a large lidded saucepan. Add the cardamom pods and
stir for 30 seconds then spray with the cooking spray and add
the onion. Stir-fry for 6 minutes until softened, then add the
korma paste, ginger paste mixture and turmeric.

3 Pour in the chopped tomatoes and stock, then bring up to
the boil. Reduce the heat to medium low, add the chicken and
simmer, partially covered, for 20 minutes, stirring occasionally.

4 Add the cherry tomatoes and cream, then simmer for
another 5 minutes until the sauce is reduced and thickened.
Remove the cardamom pods. Season to taste and squeeze
over the lime, to serve.

Tip... Serve with 50 g (1¾ oz) brown basmati rice per
person, cooked according to the packet instructions.

Ⓥ **Variation...** Instead of chicken, you could use 350 g
(12 oz) Quorn Pieces and 100 g (3½ oz) chestnut
mushrooms. Add them in step 3 and cook for 10 minutes.

Chinese red chicken

Serves 1
299 calories per serving
Takes 10 minutes to prepare,
   20 minutes to cook

3 tablespoons dark soy sauce
2 tablespoons Chinese
   cooking wine or dry sherry
1 star anise
1 cm (½ inch) fresh root
   ginger, peeled and sliced
   into matchsticks
1 clove
½ teaspoon grated orange zest
juice of ½ an orange
¼ teaspoon sugar
150 g (5½ oz) skinless,
   boneless chicken breast

Star anise, soy sauce, orange and cloves add a fragrant oriental flavour and vibrant colour to the chicken breast.

1 Put the soy sauce, Chinese cooking wine or sherry, star anise, ginger, clove, orange zest and juice and sugar in a lidded saucepan and bring to the boil. Turn off the heat, cover and leave for 5 minutes to allow the flavours to infuse.

2 Add the chicken to the pan, spoon over the sauce and return to the boil. Reduce the heat and simmer, covered, for 15–20 minutes, turning the chicken halfway through and occasionally spooning over the sauce.

3 Remove the chicken from the sauce and slice thickly on the diagonal. Serve with a little of the sauce spooned over.

Tip… Serve with steamed pak choi and 40 g (1½ oz) brown basmati rice, cooked according to the packet instructions.

Spanish chicken and rice

Serves 4
401 calories per serving
Takes 30 minutes

450 g (1 lb) skinless, boneless
  chicken breasts, cubed
calorie controlled cooking
  spray
1 onion, chopped finely
2 red peppers, de-seeded and
  cubed
1.2 litres (2 pints) hot chicken
  stock
250 g (9 oz) paella rice
150 g (5½ oz) frozen peas
salt and freshly ground black
  pepper

An all-in-one dish, Spanish style.

1 In a casserole or large saucepan, brown the chicken in the cooking spray for 3 minutes. Season and transfer to a plate.

2 Add the onion to the casserole and stir-fry for 2 minutes. Mix in the peppers and 4 tablespoons of the stock. Cover and cook for 3–4 minutes until the onion and peppers are tender.

3 Stir the rice into the juices, return the chicken to the pan and add 850 ml (1½ pints) of the stock. Simmer, uncovered, for 18 minutes until tender, stirring occasionally. Add extra stock as needed if the rice looks too dry (the finished dish should have a slightly soupy consistency).

4 Stir in the frozen peas for the last couple of minutes of cooking. Serve ladled into bowls.

🌱 **Variation...** Add a couple of cubed courgettes along with the peppers, to replace the chicken, and use vegetable stock instead.

Spice-box chicken with banana sambal

Serves 4

336 calories per serving

Takes 20 minutes to prepare, 50 minutes to cook

3 large onions, quartered

4 garlic cloves

2.5 cm (1 inch) fresh root ginger, peeled

½ teaspoon cumin seeds

½ teaspoon ground turmeric

4 cardamom pods

2 teaspoons ground coriander

2 large red chillies, de-seeded and chopped finely

2 tablespoons plain flour

1 tablespoon tomato purée

425 ml (15 fl oz) chicken stock

500 g (1 lb 2 oz) skinless, boneless chicken breasts, cubed

25 g packet fresh coriander, chopped

For the banana sambal

1 small red onion, chopped finely

½ cucumber, de-seeded and cubed

2 bananas, cubed

grated zest and juice of 1 lime

Chicken in a hot spicy sauce served with a fruity sambal.

1 Put the onions in a food processor with the garlic and ginger. Whizz until as smooth as possible and then pour in 150 ml (5 fl oz) water and whizz again.

2 Heat a large, lidded, non-stick pan. Tip in the dried spices and toast for a minute to release the flavours. Pour in the onion mixture and all but 1 teaspoon of the chopped chilli. Add the flour and tomato purée and stir well. Gradually blend in the chicken stock then cover and leave to simmer for 40 minutes, stirring occasionally, until the mixture is pulpy and the onions are completely cooked.

3 Add the chicken and half of the fresh coriander. Cover and cook very gently for 8 minutes.

4 Meanwhile, mix together all the sambal ingredients with the remaining chilli and fresh coriander and serve with the chicken.

Tips... Using puréed onion, garlic and ginger to add texture as well as flavour is a classic Indian technique. Do make sure the onions are fully cooked, though – if not, the mixture will taste a little bitter.

Serve with 50 g (1¾ oz) brown rice per person, cooked according to the packet instructions. Or try serving with one Weight Watchers mini plain naan bread per person.

Spicy jambalaya

Serves 4

365 calories per serving

Takes 20 minutes to prepare,
  30 minutes to cook

1 x 175 g (6 oz) boneless,
  skinless chicken breast,
  chopped into bite size
  chunks

3 tablespoons Cajun spice mix
  (see Tip)

calorie controlled cooking
  spray

1 medium onion, chopped

2 garlic cloves, crushed

1 fresh red chilli, de-seeded
  and chopped finely

1 yellow pepper, de-seeded
  and chopped

1 red pepper, de-seeded and
  chopped

850 ml (1½ pints) chicken or
  vegetable stock

80 g (3 oz) chorizo, sliced

400 g can chopped tomatoes

200 g (7 oz) long grain rice

salt and freshly ground black
  pepper

*Chicken, chorizo, rice and tomatoes make for a spicy filling
dish. Add more chilli if you like your food especially hot.*

1 Place the chicken breast in a small bowl and sprinkle with
the Cajun spice mix. Toss together and set aside.

2 Spray a large frying pan or wok with the cooking spray. Add
the chicken and stir-fry for 4 minutes. Stir in the onion, garlic,
chilli and peppers, and fry for another 4 minutes until they are
slightly browned and softened.

3 Add the stock, chorizo, tomatoes and rice, and then bring it
all to the boil. Turn down the heat and simmer for 20 minutes
until the rice is cooked, and has absorbed all the liquid. Season
to taste, and serve.

Tip... To make your own Cajun spice mix, combine
1 teaspoon each of paprika, ground black pepper, ground
cumin seeds, cayenne pepper, ground mustard seeds, dried
thyme, dried oregano and salt.

Stir-fried chicken

Serves 1
350 calories per serving
Takes 15 minutes

30 g (1¼ oz) Chinese thread egg noodles

1 teaspoon sesame or vegetable oil

250 g (9 oz) prepared stir-fry vegetables (e.g. spring onions, pepper, carrot, broccoli, mange tout, mushrooms)

75 g (2¾ oz) skinless, roast chicken breast, sliced into strips

¼ teaspoon ready-prepared 'fresh' root ginger

¼ teaspoon ready-prepared 'fresh' garlic

1 teaspoon ready-prepared 'fresh' coriander or parsley

¼ teaspoon Chinese five spice

1 tablespoon light soy sauce

salt and freshly ground black pepper

chopped fresh coriander or flat leaf parsley, to garnish

This is a delightful Chinese dish that is wonderfully tasty yet so easy to prepare.

1 Soak the noodles in boiling water for 6 minutes, or according to the packet instructions.

2 Meanwhile, heat the oil in a non-stick wok or large frying pan. Add all the vegetables and the chicken. Stir-fry over a high heat for 4–5 minutes. The vegetables should remain crisp, crunchy and colourful.

3 Drain the noodles thoroughly. Add them to the wok with the ginger, garlic, coriander or parsley, five spice powder and soy sauce. Stir-fry for 1–2 minutes more to heat everything thoroughly.

4 Season with salt and pepper. Serve on a warmed plate, garnished with fresh coriander or parsley.

Tip... You can buy small jars of ready-prepared fresh ingredients such as ginger, garlic and herbs – so handy for small quantities. Once opened, they can be stored in the fridge for up to six weeks.

Tandoori chicken with onion salad

Serves 4

250 calories per serving

Takes 20 minutes to prepare
+ 1 hour marinating,
25 minutes to cook

8 x 100 g (3½ oz) skinless
chicken drumsticks

2 large garlic cloves, chopped
roughly

2 tablespoons fresh mint

2 tablespoons tandoori spice
mix

1 teaspoon ground turmeric

½ teaspoon chilli powder

juice of a small lemon

6 tablespoons low fat natural
yogurt

calorie controlled cooking
spray

salt and freshly ground black
pepper

For the onion salad

1 red onion, sliced thinly

6 tomatoes, de-seeded and
cubed

4 radishes, sliced into rounds

5 cm (2 inches) cucumber,
quartered, de-seeded and
cubed

2 tablespoons lime juice

*The lightly spiced yogurt marinade helps to keep the
chicken moist and tender as it cooks.*

1 Preheat the oven to Gas Mark 6/200°C/fan oven 180°C.
Make two deep cuts on either side of each drumstick. Put the
garlic, half of the mint, the spices, lemon juice and yogurt in a
blender or food processor or use a hand held blender and make
a purée. Transfer to a shallow dish, season, add the chicken
and spoon over the marinade. Cover and leave to marinate in
the fridge for 1 hour.

2 Spray a baking tray with the cooking spray and add the
chicken. Cook in the oven for 10 minutes then turn them over
and spoon over some of the marinade. Cook for another
10–15 minutes until the chicken is cooked, there is no trace
of pink inside and the outside is golden.

3 While the chicken is cooking, prepare the onion salad.
Mix together the onion, tomatoes, radishes and cucumber.
Squeeze the lime juice over, season and sprinkle with the
remaining mint. Serve the salad with two drumsticks per
person.

Tip... Accompany with a warmed plain mini naan each.

Tex Mex chicken tortillas

Serves 4

335 calories per serving

Takes 10 minutes to prepare,
35 minutes to cook

**1 tablespoon garlic-flavoured
olive oil (see Tip)**

**225 g (8 oz) skinless, boneless
chicken breast, chopped into
chunks**

**1 bunch spring onions,
trimmed and chopped**

**1 red pepper, de-seeded and
chopped**

2 celery stalks, chopped finely

1 teaspoon chilli powder

**400 g can red kidney beans,
rinsed and drained**

**1 tablespoon chopped fresh
coriander, plus extra to
garnish**

4 medium soft tortillas

**100 g (3½ oz) low fat natural
fromage frais**

2 tomatoes, chopped finely

**½ a small red onion, chopped
finely**

**salt and freshly ground black
pepper**

*You can buy Mexican-style soft tortillas in most
supermarkets. When baked, they are crisp and delicious –
try them in this tasty recipe.*

1 Preheat the oven to Gas Mark 4/180°C/fan oven 160°C.
Heat the oil in a large frying pan and sauté the chicken for
3–4 minutes, until sealed and browned. Add the spring onions,
pepper, celery and chilli powder and cook for a few more
minutes, stirring, until softened.

2 Tip the beans into the frying pan and add the coriander. Mix
well and season with salt and pepper.

3 Lay the tortillas on a work surface and divide the filling
equally between them. Roll them up, lay them in a baking dish
and bake for 20–25 minutes.

4 Meanwhile, mix together the fromage frais, tomatoes and
onion and season with salt and pepper. Chill until ready to
serve.

5 Transfer the tortillas to warmed plates. Top each one with
a spoonful of the fromage frais mixture and sprinkle with
chopped coriander. Serve at once.

Tip... If you don't want to buy garlic-flavoured oil just for
this recipe, use olive or vegetable oil and add a crushed
garlic clove along with the spring onions.

Index

Other titles in the Weight Watchers Mini Series

ISBN 978-0-85720-932-0

ISBN 978-0-85720-935-1

ISBN 978-0-85720-934-4

ISBN 978-0-85720-938-2

ISBN 978-0-85720-931-3

ISBN 978-0-85720-937-5

ISBN 978-0-85720-936-8

ISBN 978-0-85720-933-7

ISBN 978-1-47111-084-9

ISBN 978-1-47111-089-4

ISBN 978-1-47111-091-7

ISBN 978-1-47111-087-0

ISBN 978-1-47111-090-0

ISBN 978-1-47111-085-6

ISBN 978-1-47111-088-7

ISBN 978-1-47111-086-3

ISBN 978-1-47113-165-3

ISBN 978-1-47113-166-0

ISBN 978-1-47113-167-7

ISBN 978-1-47113-164-6

For more details please visit www.simonandschuster.co.uk